The Long Pull

George Nelson Dayton at age 25

Bruce B Dayton (signature)

The Long Pull

The Life of G. Nelson Dayton

Bruce B. Dayton & Ellen B. Green

Minneapolis • Privately Published • 2013

© 2013 by Bruce B. Dayton

All rights reserved.

For additional copies, call or write:

The Marsh
15000 Minnetonka Blvd.
Minnetonka, MN 55345
(952-930-8525)

Manufactured in the United States of America

10 9 8 7 6 5 4 3 2 1

Library of Congress Control Number: 2013909482

ISBN: 978-1-4675-8173-8 (hard cover, cloth)

Contents

	On the Title	vii
1.	Youth	2
2.	Coming of Age	18
3.	Learning Retail	32
4.	Master Manager	62
5.	Boulder Bridge Farm	94
6.	Family Man	120
7.	Presbyterian, Citizen, Philanthropist	142
8.	The Long Pull	158
9.	About Grace	180
10.	Legacy	202
	Descendants	215
	Sources	216
	Illustration Credits	219
	Index	220

On the Title

George Nelson Dayton, or "Nelson," as he was known to friends and family, joined his father and brother in operating Dayton's Dry Goods just about the time it became The Dayton Company. The *Minneapolis Journal* reported in May 1911: "The existing name no longer covers the business comprehensively." Apparently Nelson's brother, Draper, had seen a need for more comprehensive management as well. After nine years of Draper's entreaty, Nelson finally agreed to join the enterprise.

Each brother purchased one-third of the common stock of the company from their father, George, to become equal partners in the business.

Draper had moved from bricklaying to management like a shooting star; he was already running the store when Nelson joined the team. Nelson started on the sales floor selling blankets, then interned with and became superintendent, in charge of the physical plant and logistics; soon he was part of corporate management. One great tal-

On the Title

ent soon became evident: Nelson excelled in choosing, recruiting, and commissioning the best of store lieutenants. The brothers teamed up as they had during their youth, deciding each would always have the other's back. Despite their differences in age, training, and experience, their talents and personalities complemented each other in growing the business.

Sometime in 1916, Dayton's added a new position—advertising manager—to its staff. Nelson chose for the job the 27-year-old Hugh Arthur, who had served as managing editor of the *Pittsburgh Sun* before managing advertising for McCreery's. Arthur soon instigated a systematic program of advertising Dayton's in daily newspapers, by direct mail, and eventually through radio and magazines. He also designated a small portion of the budget for publicity stunts—to good advantage. Soon he became publicity director. After Draper's death in 1923, Nelson, in a move to broaden governance, named three of the department store's best men—including Hugh Arthur—to directorships, the first outside the Dayton family.

Hugh Arthur, following Nelson's example, easily recognized the talents of others. For example, he sent a young woman who had initiated research so as to develop the lucrative wedding market for Dayton's straight to Nelson, who made her the buyer for Dayton's new Brides Bureau.

When Hugh Arthur retired in 1948, Nelson noted that he had counted on Arthur personally for 25 years and owed him "a genuine debt of gratitude." Arthur had noted years before that, "For sheer brilliance, I'll take Draper, but for *the long pull,* give me G. N."

Thus, the title of this book.

The Long Pull

Josephine, Caroline, Nelson, and Draper Dayton

1

Youth

George Nelson Dayton was born on August 3, 1886, at his parents' home in Worthington, a small town in Nobles County, in southwestern Minnesota. Gifted with a love of the earth, a steady nature, and a dry wit, Nelson built his character on the example of his forebears.

Both Nelson's parents—George Draper and Emma Chadwick Dayton, staunch former citizens of the Finger Lakes region of New York State—had grown up in households steeped in Christian values and a deep love based on respect. Blessed as well with a spirit of entrepreneurship, the two had packed up their young family five years before Nelson's birth, leaving the settled orchard country of their youth for a hardly prosperous but highly promising farming village in Minnesota. The trusted envoy of eastern investors, George assumed responsibility for their interests in failing mortgages there.

Before moving their children—David Draper (called Draper), born on June 13, 1880, and Caroline Ward Dayton, born February

George Draper and Emma Chadwick Dayton (ca. 1882)

5, 1883—to Worthington, the Daytons bought a house on Fourth Avenue and 13th Street. The family arrived in April 1883 and lived there five years.

In this home, on August 3, 1886, the fifth anniversary of his grandfather David Dayton's death, George Nelson Dayton was born. Under the heading "Minor Arrivals," the *Worthington Advance* announced nine days later: "At the residence of Banker Dayton, a boy." Named for his father and his father's former pastor Rev. Harry Nelson and his missionary son William, the boy was simply "Nelson" to family members and friends.

By the time Nelson was born, George had helped organize the Worthington Board of Trade, become treasurer of the school board, established the 800-acre Dayton-Bond farm, organized the Minnesota Loan and Investment Company, and begun construction of a brick block for the Bank of Worthington. Indeed, at age 29, George Dayton was the leading businessman in Nobles County. His endeavors in banking, realty, agriculture, and as a citizen, churchman, and philanthropist formed the backdrop for Nelson's early years.

In 1888 realtor George constructed several houses for sale in his Clary Addition to Worthington. The Dayton family moved into one of them—at Grand Avenue and Okabena Street—when Nelson was two years old and stayed until he was four.

A fire threatened the family's home during the Dayton family's first year in the addition. Nelson's father wrote later:

> One night a huge haybarn, full of hay, was burning. I started for the place but observed [that] clouds of cinders, driven by a heavy wind, were coming toward our home and, it seemed probable, would set fire to our house. I returned home, told wife to gather things she desired to save, and I would rouse the children. Draper was sleeping so soundly it was difficult to waken him. Rousing him, I pulled him out of bed, stood him on his feet, and told him to dress while I woke the others.
>
> After the danger had passed, we looked around for Draper and decided he had gone out to see the fire—but found he had crawled back into bed and in the morning had no knowledge of the incident. Had our home taken fire, we would have assumed he was out and not looked again for him.

A more celebrated event was the birth of Nelson's sister Josephine Elizabeth at that address on April 26, 1889, completing George and Emma's immediate family. Though Emma must have been largely occupied with her young children, the Daytons hosted at least one party there. The *Advance* reported later that year "a splendid evening social at the residence of Geo. D. Dayton, Esq., on Tuesday last. There was a very large attendance and a pleasant time was had."

Enthusiastic Presbyterians, the Daytons measured their worth not in accumulating the goods of the world but to the extent they lived lives of Christian service. Westminster Presbyterian Church of Worthington had received George and Emma (originally a Method-

Nelson Dayton as a boy

ist) in July 1883, elected George an elder a few months after Nelson's birth, and later made him a trustee. The Daytons chose early to tithe (at least 10 percent) and considered the obligation a debt when they were financially pressed. By 1887, the family was setting "aside a definite amount to be given that year." In 1888 the Daytons pledged annual support (lasting 46 years) of missionary William Nelson in Syria.

Over the years, Emma became an officer of her local Ladies' Presbyterian Missionary, Home Missionary, and Ladies' Aid Societies, often serving ice cream and cake in rooms over the bank to raise funds. The Daytons together attended local, regional, and national church and mission-society meetings and entertained visiting ministers (often relatives) and delegates. Sometimes accompanied by their children, they took part in religious revival meetings. Emma and George (superintendent for a time) also led the Sunday school; the children attended services and Sunday school and other church events.

While active in business, community, and church activities, the Daytons put family first. After they moved to the Clary Addition, the old house on Fourth Avenue and 13th Street was rolled away, and they acquired several lots adjacent to the empty property. In 1890 they commissioned Wallace Leroy Dow to design a family home, on the expanded property at Fourth Avenue and 13th Street. The house, recently renovated to its original appearance, is now open to the public.

Dow provided the Daytons with a modified Georgian Colonial design. Its floor plan, unusual in providing a nursery with a bathroom as one of front rooms on the first floor, reflected the state of the family moving in: Nelson was 4 years old, his sister Josephine a little over a year. Draper was 10, Caroline 7.

Six months after the house was complete, George wrote in his annual birthday letter to daughter Josephine, age 2: "Last fall (Oct.) we moved into our comfortable home on Block 42 of Worthington. Your father and mother enjoy the home, are very happy in it, but not con-

The Dayton home at Fourth Avenue and 13th Street in Worthington

sciously proud of it. Let us always enjoy the good things of this life, remembering gratefully the giver of every good thing."

Set in the midst of a sweeping lawn, the house was the center for Dayton family activities for almost 12 years. Emma Dayton, previously almost invisible in the Worthington newspapers though the activities of her husband were well documented there, became more active in her church, frequently offering her home for its social gatherings. In addition, the Daytons often entertained family members and friends visiting from the East.

The four Dayton children were the center of many gatherings—birthday parties and church and school-group ice-cream socials—at the house on Fourth Avenue. Outside, they liked to play on the expansive lawn, under the front porch, and in the barn behind the house.

Emma's lap remained one of Nelson's favorite places well into his childhood. His mother said he could sit there occasionally—until his feet touched the floor. For some time after he had grown to that degree, he held his legs out straight so as not to lose his place on her lap.

All the Dayton children played with others in the neighborhood. Young Nelson liked to tag along with his older brother, Draper, whom he greatly admired. Nelson especially relished being with one older neighbor boy of the Rose family, who liked to fish and regularly supplied Nelson's mother with his catch. The *Marshall Messenger* journalist later wrote in his column "Rosecracks": "For each dozen bullheads, of specified size and in prime condition, I received ten cents—cash." The boys also enjoyed swimming at Lake Okabena, within the city of Worthington and just a few blocks from their home.

Along those lines, Maud Case Anderson, teacher and principal at Worthington High School and good friend of the family, wrote:

> The three older Dayton children visited me at different times at St. Peter . . . Nelson, I think, enjoyed that experience most. He was just learning to swim and gave me many frights in his lack of experience about a swimming hole.

We went to neighboring lakes and caught many fish, which we cooked over a bonfire on the shore. [I remember] a small boy lying on his stomach and, without much dependence on knife or fork, devouring sunfish and bass by the fireside.

My father was an importer of Percheron horses. He had a 200-foot barn, the largest Nelson had ever seen, and there he spent many hours.

In 1893, the year of Nelson's seventh birthday, his father, in anticipation of a bursting economic bubble but against the advice of eastern stockholders, incorporated his bank. Almost immediately, a national economic panic led to the closing of a competing bank across the street. This caused a run on the Bank of Worthington. Because of George's insight and a few loyal investors, the bank survived the panic. But its assets and the undivided profits of the investment company plunged: "We suffered heavy losses . . . ate bread without butter and kept our expenses at the minimum. Emma for some period took in boarders, mainly teachers in the Worthington schools, to help make ends meet."

George Dayton incorporated the Bank of Worthington in 1893.

George, who by this time had substantial interests in Minneapolis, was able, despite the economic panic, to bring in on time the construction of an eight-floor medical building (The Dayton Block) at Nicollet Avenue and Sixth Street. But he had lost a lot of money because of the panic. To recover his personal financial position, he bought the stocks of banks that survived the crash.

How much the Dayton children knew of the bank panic or of their father's investment in Minneapolis is unknown. They certainly knew teachers were living in their home, and they did learn from George some economics and entrepreneurship over the years. Eleven-year-old Draper, for example, asked to multiply a nickel to help raise money for his church, sold popcorn and turned in $40.35. He might have made more had the authorities not disallowed his attempts to sell to passengers on trains stopping in the town.

The two youngest children, Nelson and Josephine, were their parents' hope for ministry beyond that of philanthropy. George wrote in another birthday letter to Josephine:

> Six years old! Another birthday party with 12 little girls and your teacher Miss Bateman here. It is Arbor Day—the school set out three trees, and at the home the day was celebrated by setting out three rose bushes. So your mother endeavors to make the home life pleasant for the children.
>
> We have lately been thinking a good deal about Foreign Missions in our home, & your father and mother have been wondering if God wanted you for that work . . .
>
> Your mother and I are very economical in our dress, in our table, and in all our living, trying to save to give all possible for the extension of Christ's kingdom upon earth. But if we give Nelson [he was nine at the time] and Josephine to be missionaries of the cross, will it not be greater than all other gifts combined?

They did not insist upon it: "God's will be done." But the hope continued. Josephine's next birthday letter said, in part: "Seven years old! . . . We have been much interested also in seeing you endeavor to bring yourself under control. Nelson [10 years old] united with the church the first Sabbath in March, and you have repeatedly asked that you be permitted to unite."

Aware of the Daytons' high expectations of their children, principal Maud Anderson wrote later:

> Draper, Caroline, and Nelson were all excellent students but all very different in temperament. I felt at the time they were somewhat prevented from leading their own lives because their father was the town's most prominent citizen, president of the school board, and a pillar of the Presbyterian Church. The children lived under very strict regulations at home. No playmates were allowed to come in [the house] in the evening, but the hours were devoted to lessons. The family entertained very little. Sunday they all went to church and Sunday school and in the evening to young people's meeting and the evening service. No bicycles were allowed on Sunday. They might not even be parked on the porch.

Neither could the chldren play "games that could be won." But they definitely had fun there, as 12-year-old Nelson indicated in an essay published in the *Worthington Globe* in June 1898:

> How the Fourth Should Be Celebrated.
> In the morning my chum and I will get up at five o'clock and fire off our cannon under my father's bedroom window, although he said we might wish we hadn't. As we are a good deal interested in the present war with Spain, we have thought out a grand scheme for celebrating this Fourth.
>
> We have made quite a number of small ships and cannons, and moulded quite a number of bullets. We have also dug a pond in which we propose to have a battle between Spain and the United States. Of course we do not doubt that United States will win. We have a fort representing Moro Castle and a number of ships representing the United States Navy attacking Havana. First our steam

launch, the *Oregon*, will appear and fire once, and then as this will exhaust her supply, she will steam up to our provision and ammunition boat, the *Hale*, and be loaded again. A couple of Spanish ships will then come round the bend and help the fort.

We will then send forward our torpedo boat, the *Terror*, to destroy the Spanish boats, our whole fleet will next appear, bombard the fort, and secure an unconditional surrender. In the evening we will have other displays such as spinning-wheel sky rockets.

—9th Room. G. Nelson Dayton

His follow-up story, published the following August, noted:

I think my happiest vacation day was the Fourth of July. On that day we had a good deal of fun. In the evening we boys had some fun chasing the skyrocket sticks. One boy ran into a post and hurt his face quite badly. A skyrocket went the wrong way and came up toward the house where it exploded burning my mother's and sister's dresses.

On that day I also got a bicycle. At first I had to have my brother hold me up. Then I got so I could get on by the side of the porch, and what fun it was running into rosebushes and fences and under trees whose branches knocked my hat off! But I wanted to get on as other people did, so after a good many bumps I succeeded. Every evening a number of boys who have bicycles go out to the fair grounds and race around the track.

—G. Nelson Dayton

From the stories he told his sons years later, Nelson apparently had a happy youth; he never complained of restrictions. Many of his memories involved animals. At a quite young age, he loved Coal, a black terrier with a white patch on one eye. The dog yapped so much that a neighbor threw an ax at him, breaking the dog's leg. Emma created a splint and bandage, enabling the dog to heal.

Nelson also loved birds, even pigeons, and he climbed the belfry of the church he attended to see them up close. And clearly he was familiar with horses at an early age. The *Advance* reported in June 1895 that he had left by train for Philadelphia with his mother and sister Josephine and would spend the summer in New York (probably Geneva). But the next summer, when he was 13, the paper noted: "Nelson Dayton had his foot quite badly injured last week by a horse stepping on it."

That was probably one of the four or five summers that Nelson spent working for sheep farmer Alex Wilson. Nelson used his earnings of about $30 to purchase two already-bred Shropshire ewes from his employer, which he was allowed to bring home to pasture on his father's ample lawn. Nelson considered himself most fortunate when both ewes produced twins, thus giving him a flock of six. The herd ultimately grew to so many that it was put out to a neighboring farmer on shares.

Nelson remembered getting up at 5 AM with his older brother, Draper, when they were about 10 and 16 years old respectively, to walk to their father's bank and sweep the floors before it opened each day. And he told of one Halloween when several older boys found a wagon in Farmer Jones's yard and set it atop a church steeple. They took great delight in the reaction of the townspeople discovering it in such a prominent place the next day.

A year later, another group, emulating this splendid trick, went to see Farmer Jones again. The boys entered his farmyard, found the wagon, and hauled it to town. When they reached their destination, Farmer Jones arose from the back of the wagon holding a shotgun. He said, "Now boys, pull it back home." Whether Nelson played a role in either group's shenanigans, we do not know. If he did, his father did not make him "wish he hadn't."

During his early teenage years, his brother already gone to Princeton, Nelson attended picnics and parties with friends. He joined the Amphictyonic Society (a literary group, supposedly patterned after the early Greeks), making recitations on such as "Topics of the Times"

*George D. Dayton at the Bank of Worthington,
which Nelson and Draper swept every day*

and "The Ride That Saved Oregon." He also entertained the "Carrom Club" (*carrom* is defined in dictionaries as a collision and rebound, in reference to games) at the Dayton residence one Friday evening. Occasionally he traveled by train to Minneapolis, once to hear a lecture by a Dr. Hillis and at one other time, at least, with his mother and sister "Miss Carrie." Little did Nelson know then that he would soon live in that larger city.

In August 1898, the year Nelson turned 12, George sold his shares of the Bank of Worthington to give more time to his Minneapolis-area real estate interests. The Daytons' newly acquired telephone connection—the *Globe* listed them among the first subscribers for both business and home lines—helped George to keep in close touch with the larger city to the northeast. Still, Nelson wrote later: "Father used to [go] up to Minneapolis part of every week. He usually got back about

2 AM Saturday morning. Most of the time I got up and went down to the train and carried his grip home for him."

In 1900, the year Nelson turned 14, his father was still involved enough in Worthington to chair its celebration of the "First 4th of the 20th Century," including music, fireworks, parades, sports, and awards for best-decorated homes and businesses. Certainly Nelson and the other members of the family also participated in these events.

Earlier that year, the family had joined about 900 other churchgoers and citizens at the dedication of the substantial new Westminster Presbyterian Church of Worthington. George had served as chair of the building committee, and he continued to be one of its most enthusiastic fundraisers. A list of those contributing to the organ fund upon the new church's debut included every member of the Dayton family. Nelson gave five dollars.

But by 1901 Nelson's father had acquired considerable footage on Nicollet Avenue in Minneapolis, enough to begin construction of another business block—this one at the corner of Seventh and Nicollet. Six years earlier, on September 6, 1895, a passerby had spotted flames licking the top of a cupola of Westminster Presbyterian Church, on that corner. Firefighters saved only the shell. Five months later the congregation voted to rebuild there, but three trustees, including William Donaldson of the Minneapolis retailing family, trekked to Worthington and urged George to buy the site for development.

In the first week of April 1896, George sealed the deal at the church's asking price—$165,000. Five years later, Nelson's brother, Draper, spent his last summer home from Princeton working as a bricklayer at the construction site. George, wishing to secure a major tenant for the building, had helped finance two young men in moving Goodfellow's Dry Goods, the fourth largest such store in the city, from Third Street to his building at Seventh and Nicollet.

With the "Grand Opening" of the new store set for June 1902, the Daytons decided to move to the city. On May 2, the *Worthington Ad-*

Westminster Presbyterian Church on the corner of Nicollet Avenue and Seventh Street in Minneapolis, later the site of Dayton's Department Store

vance reported: "Geo. D. Dayton loaded his household goods in a [railroad] car Monday for Minneapolis." The newspaper announced later that the Dayton family boarded the train for Minneapolis on July 14.

Nelson wrote 40 years later: "Father sold our house down there to Charlie [Smallwood's mother, Florence Moulton Smallwood]. We had previously bought another house in which we lived for a while. Mother, Father, and Josephine moved up to Minneapolis . . . Caroline was at Wellesley that year. I stayed down and worked for Alex Wilson . . . and didn't come up until about September 15. I was 16 that summer."

Nelson Dayton upon graduation from high school

2

Coming of Age

Nelson Dayton, soon to be 16, probably had mixed feelings about the Dayton family's move to Minneapolis. Certainly aware of his father's business activities and the family's need to move on, he may have looked forward to the adventures of living in a large city. But in Minneapolis he could not stand in an open field, feel the earth crumble in his hands, ride on a mower, or pat down a sheep or a cow, though he could care for his father's horses there. In any event, he was in no hurry to get to the city.

So, during that summer of 1902, Nelson stayed in southwestern Minnesota, working on the farm of Alex Wilson, two miles outside Worthington. Later he wrote that you could "see the Wilson farm from the railroad tracks . . . about a mile and a half away."

Eager to be close to his expanding business interests, Nelson's father had eased the pain of leaving Worthington for his family by building a new house—similar in design but more modest in size—in Minneapolis. As noted by the *Minneapolis Journal* on February 27, 1901, George had sold the Dayton Block (medical building) to former governor John S. Pillsbury, in partial payment taking 80 unimproved lots in John T. Blaisdell's revised addition. Putting most of the lots on the market, George set aside at least one for the new Dayton home on Blaisdell. By this time son Draper was finishing up at Princeton, and daughter Caroline was at Wellesley.

After working on the Wilson farm that summer, Nelson took the train to Minneapolis to live with his family at 2020 Blaisdell Avenue and finish his secondary education at Central High School. In the months following, he became familiar to the employees of his father's store, who thought of him as "the farmer son." His brother, Draper, was "the city son" who worked at the store. Joe McNamara, a plumber working at the Dayton home, remembered seeing Nelson for the first time—in overalls, coming in from watering his father's horses in the barn in back of the house.

In May 1903, at the end of his junior year in high school, Nelson, with his parents and sister Josephine, was received by certificate into the First Presbyterian Church of Minneapolis, at Portland Avenue and 19th Street. Probably the family visited several Presbyterian congregations before deciding which to join. Years later when that church closed, George and Emma joined Nelson and his family at Westminster Presbyterian in downtown Minneapolis. Nelson attended that church, which exists today, for the rest of his life.

In the summer of 1903 Nelson again worked on Alex Wilson's farm, and the next summer, after his senior year and graduation from high school, he did so again. On the eve of his 18th birthday (August 3, 1904) his mother, Emma, wrote him from Minneapolis:

My dear Nelson:
I have planned for some time to spend the summer with you, but owing to Papa's contemplated trip east and Caroline's guest, I concluded I had better stay home. Then the length of your days [is] such that we wouldn't have seen much of each other anyway, unless your mower has a seat for two, which I doubt.

Yesterday I spent in the kitchen in your behalf and last evening sent you some of the fruits of my labor. We hardly thot best to wait until tonight before mailing it for fear there would be some delay. Papa took them to the office and said the first thing the clerks did was to throw them behind them on the floor. As the Margaritas [cookies] were brittle and the candy soft, I feel quite doubtful of their condition by the time they reach you. But whatever that may be, it will show my love and thot for you, which was what we wanted. All three of the girls helped me in one way and another, so it was a combination affair.

We would all rejoice in your presence in the home tomorrow, and would count it a privilege to contribute to your happiness, but cheerfully submit to the inevitable, and in doing so admire you for your manly pluck and perseverance. You are a great comfort to us, my boy. We expect good things of you and feel you will not disappoint us. God has been good to us in our children, and we are glad and thankful. Tomorrow can be a happy day for you even tho you are alone in the field, for you can know that we are all following you with loving thots and wishes.

Papa told me to write you that on your return you could select 10 swine of the Statesman series as a gift from your parents. That will make 20, counting the 10 promised in June.

I enclose your report card, which came in yesterday. We are all pleased with it . . .

After a few bits of news about family friends, she concluded: "'May God richly bless and keep you and bestow upon you all that is for your own best good' is the prayer of your loving Mother."

Where Nelson kept those 20 swine (perhaps the 10 promised in June were a gift in celebration of his high-school graduation) is a mystery, but as he spent several subsequent summers at the Wilson farm, he may have tended to them there.

After high school, Nelson attended classes at Macalester College in St. Paul, a Presbyterian liberal arts school that his parents had supported for at least a decade. After two years at Macalester, however, he decided to transfer to the University of Minnesota School of Agriculture, known to many as "the farm school." Thirty years later, Nelson wrote to his son Bruce, "I got out of school in the spring of 1907 . . . In a few days I signed a note to Father for $100,000 to buy Oak Leaf Farm."

For 4,800 acres of land in Anoka County near Coon Lake, northwest of Minneapolis, Nelson paid $20 an acre ($96,000), his father advancing him $4,000 in cash as well. According to Deborah Morse-Kahn in *Boulder Bridge Farm,* "The farmhouse was spartan: no running water or electricity, the rooms being lit by oil lamps." Nelson continued in his letter: "We spent a lot of money out there buying stock, fencing, and making various improvements. I kept signing notes to him for this money and for interest."

Even later, Nelson wrote Bruce's brother Ken, "I didn't make enough money off the farm to take care of the improvements, taxes, etc., and kept giving Father notes for these various items. We ran a big herd of Holstein cows, some beef cattle, and about 300 sheep out there." Oak Leaf's chief crop was wire grass, used in making rope and brooms.

Nelson remembered struggling with the huge farm, which he worked himself for five years. But he also told his sons of driving with horse and wagon from the farm to town (probably Anoka) for a little fun on Saturday nights. When he wanted to go home, he simply wrapped the reins around his hand and lay down on the wagon seat to sleep. The horses always took him right home.

Through Nelson's years on Oak Leaf Farm, his father and brother, Draper, who had joined Goodfellow's (soon Dayton Dry Goods Company) straight out of Princeton, tried many times to persuade him to join the retail business. Much attached to his country roots, Nelson demurred—that is, until he planned to marry.

According to *A Bliss Genealogy,* Nelson's sister Caroline, a traveling YWCA secretary, in 1910 or 1911 met Grace Caruthers Bliss at a

Coming of Age

Grace Caruthers Bliss in Mitchell, South Dakota

meeting of the YWCA, location unknown. Caroline knew enough of Grace, a coed at Dakota Wesleyan University in Mitchell, South Dakota, to recommend her to Nelson.

Like her eventual mate, Grace Caruthers Bliss was descended through her father's line from an Englishman—Thomas Bliss, a blacksmith seeking "a better life of the spirit" in America in the early 17th century. He settled early in Hartford in what later became Connecticut. Among Grace's other ancestors were Margaret Lawrence Bliss, remembered in the Bliss and Margaret Streets still found in Springfield, Massachusetts; Mary Bliss Parsons (married to a fur trader), who went on trial for but was acquitted of witchcraft in 1675; Robert Woods Bliss of the U.S. Diplomatic Service, later assistant secretary of state; and Gen. Tasker Howard Bliss, U.S. Army chief of staff turned militant pacifist.

Grace's father, Cortis James Bliss (1861–1929), a tall, handsome man, was half itinerant Methodist minister and half horse-trader, from Richford, Vermont. Her mother was Emma Gamble Bliss, likely also from Vermont. They moved to South Dakota but returned to Vermont when Emma Bliss became unhappy with "pioneer" life. Back in Vermont, the Blisses took the death of their firstborn, in about 1885, as a sign they should return west. Their son Frank Hartsough was born in 1887; and on February 15, 1890, in Wessington Springs, South Dakota, they welcomed to the family a daughter—Grace Caruthers Bliss.

In Dakota, Cortis Bliss conducted Sunday services, presumably Methodist, riding on horseback to various small settlements. But his real business was horse-and-cattle trading—he bought animals from the more western states and shipped them east, possibly in an informal partnership with his brother, Franklin, who lived in Omaha, Nebraska. Cortis also owned a farm in Vermont, to which he returned twice a year to harvest apples and make maple syrup.

Grace's mother, Emma, died in Parkston, South Dakota, in August 1892, when Grace was still a toddler. Within a couple of years, her father married a distant cousin, Addie Corliss, probably also from Vermont, who reared Grace and Frank from that time. The Blisses then lived in Mitchell, where Grace attended high school before going to Dakota Wesleyan University there.

Described as a small, beautiful woman, a devout Methodist, and a fine human being, Grace was highly intelligent, had great energy, and was unusually generous, kind, and sympathetic. No wonder Nelson was taken with her. But according to *The Bliss Genealogy,* which credits the details of the following account to Grace's stepmother, their courtship was not without its difficulties:

Grace

The logistics of meeting and courting a girl who lived hundreds of miles away was formidable in the early years of the [20th] century, when railroads were the rapid means of travel . . .

Nelson had to take an overnight train from Minneapolis, Minnesota, to Mitchell, South Dakota, to be presented to Grace in the presence of her parents. And he had to take that trip many times, spending about 12 tedious hours on the train each way, in exchange for brief time in her company . . .

There being no night life to speak of outside the fast urban centers (even much of that not suitable for respectable young women), their dates may have included some chaperoned social activities but usually were "calls" in the Bliss parlor with at least one parental chaperone at home. Properly, the call ended promptly at 10 PM.

One hot-blooded night, Nelson overstayed until 10:30, possibly the night he proposed but more likely the night Grace accepted; surely they were separate occasions, for a decorous girl in those days would not have leaped at the first chance. Nelson had the profound decency to call on Grace's father the next morning to apologize for his headstrong behavior, thus confirming the parents' confidence in his moral values.

Whenever the engagement became official—not before Grace had been invited to Minneapolis to meet Nelson's parents as a matter of both propriety and record—she insisted on completing her Bachelor of Arts degree before the wedding, thus suggesting that she received her ring no later than her senior year, 1911–12 . . . Whether Nelson admired this forward view or merely indulged his bride-to-be . . . he abandoned his wish that Grace drop out of college to marry.

Yet Grace didn't dally after commencement, despite the long engagements typical of the period. She set the wedding date for October 1, 1912, allowing minimal time to produce essential trousseau items—volumes of handmade batiste petticoats and embroidered pillowcases, for example, that were supposed to be made by loving hands at home, not purchased. Since Grace and her stepmother were skilled with the needle, it can be assumed that the bride arrived in Minneapolis confident that her trousseau would stand inspection by the most critical eye.

Coming of Age

Grace (above, in detail from her class photo) graduated from Dakota Wesleyan University. Her name is the eighth inscribed on a boulder still on the campus.

Actually, Nelson told his sons, Grace may have wished to set the wedding date earlier. He told her that while he knew it was the woman's prerogative to choose the date, as a farmer he could not possibly consent to a wedding before the harvest—not before October 1, 1912. That was the date she chose.

The genealogy continues with a description of the wedding as an occasion posing "a logistical problem."

> [The problem was] not the ceremony, which probably was held in Mitchell's [First Methodist Episcopal] Church, to which the Blisses belonged (early in the marriage, Grace transferred her church membership to Westminster Presbyterian, but not until after the young couple had, so to speak, shopped other Protestant churches and agreed that Nelson's [church] was to be theirs).
>
> And [the problem was] not the reception, which was held at the Bliss house. The problem was where the Dayton family could stay. The respectable women of the wedding party couldn't be put up in the local hotel that, like all prairie hotels then, catered to drummers [traveling salesmen] and lesser nomads. Further, the Dayton family had to trace by railroad Nelson's courtship route to attend and return home.
>
> George D. Dayton's neat solution was to hire a bedroom Pullman car, which was hitched to the regular overnight train, thus providing transportation and quarters for his family and also for the bride and groom, who were aboard when the train pulled out on its return trip to Minneapolis.

Nelson and Grace Dayton returned to Minneapolis after a short wedding trip to live at 2100 Blaisdell, next door to his parents, in a house purchased from the Hendricks, for which Nelson signed another note to his father.

The new Mrs. Dayton, with strong humanitarian bent, fit easily into Nelson's larger family. The newlyweds received the following letter, undated as to year (9/28/19--) but penned from the Buckwood Inn, Shawnee-on-Delaware, Pennsylvania:

Dear Nelson & Grace,

First, let me thank Nelson for bringing Grace into the family—then let me thank Grace for so sweetly adapting herself to the new surroundings. We are glad for you both and hope the years, as they pass, will bring to you more and more of happiness and of the joy that will become eternal.

I need not say that we find increasing pleasure in Grace taking on the burdens and privileges of "service" . . .

"God bless you both and your household" is the prayer of your affectionate Father.

Both Grace and Nelson had completely new lives—Grace, who had been a student in a small town on the prairie, was now an urban wife and homemaker. Nelson, who had been a bachelor living alone on a farm, was now a husband with a home in the city and—because

Nelson and Grace's first home, at 2100 Blaisdell Avenue, Minneapolis

of his brother's and father's persistence—a completely new job to boot.

In October 1910 Nelson had finally agreed to his election as a director of Dayton's Dry Goods. Early in 1911, the year before his marriage, he became a vice president of his father's retail company. In May, George had acquired the last of the property between Seventh and Eighth Streets needed for the store to front a full block on Nicollet Avenue. In July 1911, the business had become, officially, The Dayton Company. Looking to their need for more executive talent—now more than ever—George and Draper, after many years of urging, finally persuaded Nelson Dayton to join them in active operation of the business, which he did that August.

Later Nelson wrote: "My brother kept after me to come into the store and finally, in the summer of 1911, I came . . . Father sold one-third of the store to Draper and one-third to me, taking our notes for $100,000. That was a damned good buy . . . [He gave] one-twelfth to each of our two sisters; and Father, Mother, and the D. I. [Dayton Investment] Company held the balance of the common stock."

By 1912, Nelson, having completed his formal education, chosen first to farm, then to take a new, mercantile, career path and marry, had set his future professional and domestic course.

The ultimate disposal of Nelson's Oak Leaf property (and that of his father's agricultural interests in Anoka County) is not known. Nelson must have held onto the Oak Leaf farm for a time, however, as a ca. 1915 newspaper article on farming in the Anoka area carried a photo showing "the back soil being turned by a plow drawn by a caterpillar traction engine on the farm of G. Nelson Dayton."

At any rate, when Nelson joined Dayton's Department Store in 1912, he was highly leveraged financially. With a one-third interest in the business, however, his ducks were in a row to resolve that. And, as he delved into the business of merchandising, he set aside, for the time being, his dream of operating a great farm.

Goodfellow's Dry Goods became Dayton's Dry Goods and, in 1911, The Dayton Company, when Nelson joined the store (above, in 1917).

3

Learning Retail

Nelson Dayton, a farmer at heart, made his debut in merchandising because of his brother's persistent urging. Nelson's wife, Grace, often noted that Nelson's father, a developer at heart, would "rather make a dollar in real estate than two dollars in retail." Nelson may rather have made a dollar in farming, yet once he chose to enter The Dayton Company, he unreservedly threw his energies into retail.

His father had entered the business simply because he needed a major tenant to draw traffic "downtown" from what in 1902 was the city's center of commerce. After a prospective tenant folded, George persuaded J. B. Mosher and George Loudon to move Goodfellow's Dry Goods from Third Street to his new, six-story building on Seventh and Nicollet—former site of the Westminster Presbyterian Church, which had burned in a fire. Each of the store's partners—Dayton, Loudon, and Mosher—took a one-third interest in the venture.

Still, "I had no thought or idea of being a merchant," George said. And he was not—until one active partner's unscrupulous dealings and

Draper Dayton, salutarian of his high school class, five years before joining the store

the other's fear in the face of initial losses led to George's sole ownership of the store.

From the beginning, however, George must have expected some long-term, more personal involvement, at least through his oldest son. The *Minneapolis Journal* reported on June 25, 1902, that Draper Dayton, "the junior member of the firm, graduated this month from Princeton University, 'cum laude' . . . has already entered with enthusiasm upon his career as a [department store] man. It is his desire to begin at the bottom and work his way up and thus become thoroughly acquainted with all the details of the business."

Learning Retail

George needed Draper to attend to those details. Goodfellow's faced stiff competition from L. S. Donaldson and Company, Minnesota's leading department store, operating in the "Glass Block" at Sixth and Nicollet. Only heavy advertising coupled with a variety of merchandise priced for value and good service could bring customers regularly to a place that, in most minds, was not only on the wrong side of the street but also much farther from downtown than its competitor.

The new store, after its grand opening, did provide the goods and service, and its clientele bought enough to more than double Goodfellow's previous annual sales, to $600,000 the first year in its new location. Within two years, George bought out his two partners, one "crooked," the other scared. George wrote later: "It was very risky, but really there was nothing for us to do but go ahead with the store. We lost money, but we gained experience. I kept track of losses until they

A display window about the time Draper Dayton joined Goodfellow's Dry Goods

passed $100,000. Then I said, 'I don't want to know the loss. We are going to make this win.'"

But the store was not a losing investment. The early operating losses, while requiring from George a total of $300,000, stemmed from growing the business. It expanded by more than 30 percent in 1903, with increases of 7 percent, 11 percent, then 29 percent each year until 1906, when it showed a profit. It made money in every subsequent year.

Draper Dayton joined the executive roster in 1903, the year the corporation became Dayton Dry Goods Company. A *"Special* to the

George D. Dayton bought out his two partners and became sole owner of the store.

A double sign marked the passage of Goodfellow's to Dayton's Dry Goods.

Dry Goods Economist" on May 26, 1903, listed Draper, who had interned for a year in positions ranging from bundle boy to merchandising manager, as secretary and treasurer of the firm. From the first he was determined to make the new Dayton Dry Goods the leading department store in town.

The new store offered everything from silks, gloves, leather goods, and umbrellas to men's furnishings on the first floor; millinery to dresses, corsets, and infants' wear on the second; and carpets, draperies, blankets, and furniture to an art gallery and tea room on the third.

The millinery department, 1903

It sold tiny lots of stock to customers to promote ownership and patronage, and it offered forwarding-thinking employees benefits such as a full week's vacation with pay. In this manner did the store in a few short years gain a loyal following of customers and employees.

George, as president, set the initial tone of the store with the help of his son Draper, who was open to fresh ideas and believed that a store could cater to the popular *and* to the well off. He rejected arbitrary limits to its market potential. Draper was, according to his father, ever "thinking, planning how to strengthen the points of our service, how to maintain better assortments, how to secure choicer stocks, how to make the public who came to the store more happy so that they would wish to come again."

Draper recognized that to serve many, the store must depend on many. Thus he strategized with his father in assembling a group of talented merchants eager to share their individual expertise yet willing to work together to make the business succeed. So, from the store's earliest years, a team of fine merchants tested and refined Draper's merchandising philosophy and strategy.

Happy with the store's growing bottom line (see chart, pages 206–207) and recognizing in son Draper many of the traits serving well in his own career, George in 1906 named Draper general manager. In effect turning over the store's management to his eldest son, George continued to aid in the real estate and financial aspects of the business, while maintaining his office and a regular presence in the store—as well as serving as its spokesperson.

The competition wasn't going away in the face of new management; in fact, it was getting closer. In March and November 1906, L. S. Donaldson announced plans to expand by building an addition at Nicollet and Seventh, kitty-corner from Dayton's. In January 1907 came Donaldson's announcement of plans for a ten-story building there.

Dayton's intended to more than keep up with—in fact, to surpass—its competition, and though its executive didn't speak of it, their intention almost from the beginning was to make Dayton's the leading department store in the city. With George in charge of real estate, the store took over the remaining first-floor space of its building in September 1907, remodeling that as well as the basement and second floors. The *Minneapolis Journal* confirmed his earlier choice of property for investment, noting that the store had "brought the shopping public up the avenue and paved the way for other shops until now Dayton's store can be said to be in the very heart of the shopping district."

In 1909, Dayton's Dry Goods was keeping a steady eye on L. S. Donaldson's as Draper and George worked to carry out their own initiatives—specifically, in March, the opening of a "complete new basement store" to serve the "very large number of persons in this city who wish to buy dependable, service-giving, and creditable merchandise but cannot afford, or don't want to pay, more than is absolutely necessary to secure these qualities."

Pilot Glenn Curtiss exhibited his "Curtiss Airship" at Dayton's and later used it to fly goods to the store.

That idea exemplified the basic merchandising philosophy followed by all the Dayton stores through the years—to take as big a "slice of the pie" as possible. The basement store aimed at lower prices, the upstairs store at the middle and upper levels. And six months after the basement opening, the store announced that it would extend its "building at Seventh Street and Nicollet Avenue to a frontage on Eighth Street and the front of Mary Place [La Salle Avenue]."

Then Dayton's paused to share its vision of the future with customers in the first of a series of innovative publicity stunts featuring recent inventions. Impressed by pilot Glenn Curtiss, who had just won a race with his biplane in Rheims, France, George invited exhibition in Minneapolis of the "Curtiss Airship," a stock biplane designed for commercial use.

While attracting customers with the opportunity to see something new and different, Dayton's Dry Goods never let up on its work towards expansion. But neither did its competition. In mid-March 1910, Donaldson's announced plans for a five-story annex. Two weeks later the *Journal* reported that Dayton's was squaring its block by "adding 10,500 feet floor space."

In early May 1910, George was able to obtain the one missing piece for expansion—a 100-year lease (costing $3 million) for property at the corner of Eighth and Nicollet. This acquisition completed for the store the frontage of a full block on Nicollet Avenue. (Donaldson's acquired the full block from Sixth to Seventh Streets six years later.)

While Dayton's would not take control of its block until 1911, employees (by this time 750) filling the aisles in a meeting at the store cheered when they heard the news. "We have now a building four times as large as we had eight years ago. The volume of business has increased seven times," George told them.

Dayton's at Seventh and Nicollet

In March 1911, the store opened its annex (another 215 feet towards its goal of being the first to control a full block on Nicollet) in time to celebrate its ninth anniversary. And in May it took control of the Eighth and Nicollet property, announcing that construction to complete the Nicollet frontage would begin the following March.

With an increasingly burning desire to lead in sales as well as in its presence on Nicollet Avenue—that is, to surpass Donaldson's—Dayton's pledged to provide an even greater variety of goods and services, including delivery of packages to the train station for commuters and the promise that "What's Wrong, We'll Right."

In May 1911, too, the *Journal* announced that, because "the existing name no longer covers the business comprehensively," the Dayton Dry Goods Company was changing its name to The Dayton Company, effective July 15. This was the point at which George and Draper, after nine years of entreaty, finally convinced Nelson to join the enterprise.

With each taking (and paying for) one-third of the common stock of the company (see chapter 2), brothers Draper and Nelson became equal partners in the business. Holding one another in great affection, they teamed up as they had in their youth. At the start of their store partnership, they decided each would always support the other so as to present a united front to associates. Their personalities complemented each other despite their differences in age, training, and experience.

Draper had become general manager of the store five years earlier, when he was just 26 years old. He was, according to his father, "an able organizer, a keen conservative financier, a genius in planning campaigns of all kinds. He had a marvelous memory for figures, names, layouts of stores, and details of management; he had a natural intuition for merchandise."

Outgoing and mercurial, Draper clearly was the more dominant brother, even in the community. John R. Van Dewlap, who served with Draper as a director of the First National Bank of Minneapolis, wrote that Draper was "universally respected and admired: His friends

Horse-drawn wagons delivering goods from Dayton's were a common sight in the first three decades of the twentieth century.

were legion; he had no enemies . . . it may safely be said of him, without detracting from the merits of any of his contemporaries, that he was the most conspicuous figure of his age in the business circles of the community."

Brother Nelson, by this time 28 years old, was the more quiet and steady partner. Making the rounds through the receiving, wrapping, delivery, lace, pay-roll, auditing, and operations departments, he also took a turn at buying and merchandising. Starting as a buyer "in blankets," a department well behind the sales of its biggest competitor, Nelson bought the best he could and sold them at cost until word of mouth backed by value built customer loyalty.

After his debut in blankets, Nelson worked in the office of the general superintendent, and he soon took that position, assuming responsibility for the store's physical plant and logistics in 1915. He also helped recruit new people for key positions in the store.

Nelson had more in common with his father than many might have supposed—his insight in dealing with land and property, his tendency for analysis, and his aptitude for picking the right people to do the work he needed done. And the retiring and unostentatious "Mr. G. N." had the drive to help Draper assemble the executive staff needed to shape Dayton's into a leading mercantile concern.

Nelson's ability to manage through delegation was perhaps his greatest executive asset: "I don't claim to know how it should be done," he told his associates. "That's your job." And in every project he took on, Nelson demonstrated and encouraged initiative and independence in solving the problems that came up.

Draper clearly was the merchant of the two brothers. Nelson was a master in the recruitment of store managers and executives. One of these, Hugh Arthur, who became advertising manager for the Dayton enterprise, said, "For sheer brilliance, I'll take Draper, but for the long pull, give me G. N." The complementary Dayton brothers drove the company forward.

None of the Daytons relied on inspiration alone: George was a close analyst of economic trends. Draper studied every aspect of merchandising. Nelson's greater talent lay in managing the right people. All three understood and had great ambitions for the store's position in the market.

Settling into new offices on the seventh floor, the new executive team looked to the store's continuing expansion, plowing profits back into new construction, with Nelson in charge of every expansion project. Increasingly involved in other matters and with a much lesser financial interest, George, spent much less time on store affairs, though he was ready to be called upon as realtor and spokesperson.

In 1912 a new annex (sub-basement, basement, and one-story building running along the rear of the original structure), gave Dayton's its first entrance on Eighth Street. In announcing this improvement, the *Minneapolis Journal* called Dayton's "the fastest growing store in the northwest." With typical foresight and an eye toward

The 1913 annex on Eighth and Nicollet

building for tomorrow, George insisted that the one-story annex—and every further addition to the original building—be strong enough to accommodate 12 floors. In 1913 the annex was completed and the floor space further enlarged by taking over, on a rental basis, the one-story shops at the corner of Eighth and Nicollet. Dayton's now had entrances on three streets—Seventh, Nicollet, and Eighth.

At the same time, the store policy of making the customer happy grew stronger, especially as to returns: Nelson, who formulated the attitude, often said, "It isn't a question of whether the customer is right or wrong; it is a question merely of whether she thinks she is right." As a result, Dayton's developed a reputation for its generous return policy and loyal clientele.

Soon after completion of the annex, Dayton's faced with other businesses some alarming international events ultimately leading to Germany's declaration of war in Europe on August 1, 1914. Several months earlier, Draper and Nelson, reading the signs of war, had sent buyers east to purchase merchandise at low prices in anticipation of high demand, higher prices, and thus the possibility of enough profit to fatten the store's reserve fund. Retail prices did skyrocket then, providing the store with enough profit to create a reserve healthy enough to see it through even harder times and so give it an edge on the competition.

Three large Dayton's ads running in local newspapers in late summer 1914 served as a calming voice—reassuring Dayton employees and customers alike. The first two ads, placed in August, stated Dayton's faith in the economic future of the Northwest, promising to "take care of our customers." The third ad ran in September. Titled "The Silk Situation," it refuted a local report that "war means no Silk or Dye Goods here" and promised the greatest annual silk sale ever.

Dayton's delivered on its promise, and Nelson used the profits to rebuild and expand the store's reserve bond fund, later described by Harry Piper, head of Piper Jaffray, as one of the better bond accounts in town. Nelson in a lesson to his son Bruce said that Dayton's freight elevator operator, who sometimes provided Nelson with inconspicuous transportation to his office on the seventh floor, knew of his success with the fund. One day he asked, "Do you have any of the new 8 percent bonds, Mr. G. N.? I do!" Nelson thought he could better afford the risk of those bonds than the elevator man.

Before the end of 1914, the progressive management of Dayton's earned its selection over the still-larger Donaldson's as a founding member of the Retail Research Association (RRA). Lincoln Filene first conceived the idea of forming a group of leading American department stores—including Filene's of Boston, Bloomingdale's of New York, Abraham & Straus of Brooklyn, Hudson's of Detroit, and Strawbridge & Clothier of Philadelphia—to exchange operating figures and ideas. Later this group formed the Associated Merchandising Corporation (AMC), which developed a buying office in New York as well as in London, Paris, Florence, Vienna, and Tokyo. Already the fifth highest store in the RRA, Dayton's aimed to match the average operating figures of the top three stores in each category of merchandise.

The Daytons on several occasions recognized in members of the RRA/AMC staff talents valuable for their own operation. Arthur C. White, for example, was just the man they needed to follow Nelson as operating superintendent. And Dayton's hired another former AMC employee—Alan Phillips—noted for his research and ability to predict merchandising trends.

Close family friendships also resulted from the AMC alliance. The Daytons became great friends, for example, with the Webber family of Hudson's in Detroit—Dick Webber, who owned 51 percent of Hudson's stock, was Draper's age, and his brother, Oscar Webber, was Nelson's.

Demonstrating its stated faith in a growing economy, The Dayton Company continued its expansion, in the summer of 1915 announcing what was variously reported as an eight- or nine-story extension of the store—despite the war. By mid-July, construction of an eight-story addition was in progress. At the end of the year, the store announced plans for the erection of another, four-story, addition on Eighth Street, its foundation designed like the rest to carry 12 stories.

In planning for merchandise to fill the huge space, the company reserved in February 1916 a special train car for the use of Dayton buyers traveling east. To finish construction of the addition and complete purchase of still another 50-foot frontage on Eighth Street, the company borrowed $800,000 on a mortgage funded by New York Life Insurance Company.

The Dayton Company sometime in 1916 added a new position—advertising manager—to its staff. Recruited for the job was 27-year-old Hugh Arthur, who had served as managing editor of the *Pittsburgh Sun* before managing advertising for McCreery's. He instigated a systematic program of advertising in daily newspapers, by direct mail, and later through radio and magazines, and designated a small portion of the budget for publicity stunts.

Always cognizant of the role the staff played in the success of the store, the Daytons instructed the new advertising department to announce two days before Christmas 1916 that, as was the usual annual custom, sales personnel would share in a profit distribution, figured at 2 percent (up to $35) of the sales of each clerk during the holiday season. Other workers would receive $5 or $10 each, according to their length of service.

Two days after Christmas that year, the Daytons sought to stop a potential impediment to full store expansion with a full-page ad in the *Journal*. The ad opposed a proposal to extend Mary Place (La Salle Avenue) from Eighth through Seventh Streets, asking whether such an extension at public expense would do more harm for one business than good for another in the city, while making a mess of traffic to boot. It emphasized the positive effects for the city that the Daytons' plan would bring. The argument was convincing, the proposal for extension was dropped, and the store realized its 12-story vision three decades later.

Two months after this victory, disaster struck. At about 1:00 AM on Saturday, February 17, 1917, George Jones, a night watchman, discovered flames in the two-story Dayton building at the corner of Eighth Street and Nicollet, the site of the silk and shoe department as well as of several shops. Engine Company No. 23's hose cart, racing to the scene from Hennepin and 36th Street, overturned on the way. All the other Minneapolis firefighters on duty, using all the firefighting equipment in the city, battled a 48-mile-per-hour gale and below-zero temperatures for three hours before bringing under control the flames destroying Dayton's shoe and silk stock and putting the whole retail district at risk.

Firewalls, steel doors, and a force of Dayton employees helped firefighters keep the blaze from spreading to the original Dayton Building, to newer construction, and to other buildings downtown. Shoe-stock loss alone was estimated early at between $300,000 and $500,000. But

The morning after the 1917 fire at the Dayton store

smoke and water damage affected to some extent much of the stock in the rest of the store. In addition, water filled the sub-basement to 11 feet, covering the heating plant. The 600 employees reporting to work Saturday morning were dismissed "for the day," but on Monday, another ad announced the store closed until further notice.

George Dayton, who had sloshed through waist-high water to assess the damage before Nelson and Draper returned with 30 department heads from a buying trip, announced the fire's effect but noted: "The last of the water was pumped out of the basement yesterday, and by noon we had fires under the boiler . . . we hope to . . . resume business soon."

Nelson and Draper rallied with a quickly thought-out program for recovery, put into action even as adjustors surveyed the remains. Business did resume on the following Monday, February 26. Dayton personnel had telegraphed shoe suppliers before the fire was out, to explain the store's need for replacement stock. As the managers returned and further damage became evident, other suppliers responded as rapidly, in some cases putting on extra shifts to manufacture the emergency orders.

As a result, the shoe department opened with all new stock, and the rest of the store offered tremendous bargains plus the service of "several hundred extra salespeople" in a sale unlike any other. Thousands of customers enjoyed greatly reduced prices on slightly damaged, usable items as well as on special merchandise brought in for the sale.

The ad campaign, the quick recovery, the sale—and the announcement that all 1,500 employees would be paid for the days the business was closed—resulted in immeasurable good will and respect for the store. With its competition growing, however, the store could not rest: L. S. Donaldson had just a few months earlier announced its expansion into the former quarters of the Gimbel-Zimmer Company, thus reaching a full block's frontage on Nicollet. The Dayton Company, in reporting assessment of the fire damage, took the occasion to invite construction bids for its planned frontage on Eighth Street.

Seizing the tragedy of the fire as an opportunity to recreate an area of the business that was rapidly growing, Draper and Nelson offered store-trained designer C. J. Larson the chance to plan for and rebuild its "bargain basement," which Larson immediately renamed the "Downstairs Store." With reconstruction, the basement area of all the buildings was completely revamped. Offering real, fresh bargains—not items that didn't sell elsewhere—the Downstairs Store was a totally separate operation, in competition with the store above it. Eventually it became, on its own, the third largest department store in town.

As the planning and construction progressed, however, the country's attention turned to a disaster of larger importance. Before the end of February 1917, German submarines sank 151 neutral ships, two of them American, in an area near the British Isles. In the first week of April, Congress declared a state of war. Though formal declara-

New construction after the fire, 1917

tion against Austria did not occur until December, several young Dayton's employees immediately enlisted in the U.S. military. Others were drafted, and 84 employees served before the war was over. Considering these departed employees part of the family, the store sent them news of the home base along with gifts and money.

On the executive front, Nelson, who was active in the Minneapolis Retailers Association, traveled to Washington, likely by train, to represent that body at a July 10 meeting with the "economy board of the council of national defense." According to an unidentified Minneapolis newspaper clipping, the meeting was expected to be "of great importance relative to wartime mobilization of all resources" and "the retail merchants will be asked to advise the council as to the best means for organizing for high efficiency." Topics for discussion included, among others, "the cutting down of unnecessary deliveries, discontinuance of the practise of sending goods to homes of prospective purchasers on approval, employment of women in positions formerly held exclusively by men, and working hours for men and women."

The store turned to itself for happier news, celebrating with flair the graduation in 1917 of 28 employees from a three-year course of study initiated by Ima Winchell Stacy. One local newspaper noted that the course was required of "every clerk . . . stock boy, or other employee" who had not finished high school or worked at the store long enough to "have acquired education through experience." The diplomas indicated "proficiency in spelling, penmanship, arithmetic, composition, salesmanship, and knowledge of textiles."

> December 15, 1917
> A year ago today was the largest day the Store had up to then.
> Let us every one strive today to pass that record.
> Geo. D. Dayton

> **YOU DID IT.**
> Saturday's was the biggest day's business in the history of the Store. Thank you.
> Geo. D. Dayton, Pres.

*Dayton's clerks set a new record in sales in December 1917—
and shared in the profits.*

The Dayton Company planned social events for its employees, too. From the time of the store's opening, its management, including Nelson, sometimes instigated and usually attended picnics, parties, and impromptu entertainments for workers, many of them at the store. Some of these pursuits became eagerly anticipated annual events.

Of course, the war was never completely out of mind. On January 17, 1918, the store announced that employees would be paid for the ten Mondays they missed work as the store closed to conserve coal for the war effort. Other efforts included providing space in the store as a headquarters for the acceptance and distribution by the Red Cross of clothing items such as sweaters, socks, and hospital gowns made by volunteers at home.

Because of such activities, the employees displayed great *esprit de corps* during the war. In an effort to keep in closer contact those both at home and at war, Nelson and Draper decided that the store would do well to produce a regular newsletter. On July 10, 1918, it published Vol. I, No. 1, of *The Daytonews*—two cents a copy. Dayton's joined with several other establishments declaring new, shorter hours (9:00 AM–5:30 PM), likely a concession to the war. In October the store adopted a suggestion for a "Daily Minute of Prayer . . . for our country and a sorrowing world."

During the same week, a Dayton Company ad entreated customers: "The U.S. War Industries Board Asks You to Do Your Christmas Shopping Now, That All the Man and Woman Power Possible Be Conserved for Government Requirements. We not only 'second' the request of the government authorities, but we will surrender part of our profits to make it worth your while to purchase [war-time] gifts now."

The store's presentation of goods was more than practical, however. Starting with employees, Dayton's promised in the November 10 *Daytonews*, a "mad bedlam of fun—a gloom-chaser deluxe," in an after-hours store fair introducing personnel to new merchandise, starting from the top floor and ending at the grand new Downstairs Store.

The very next day an armistice ended the war, and Dayton's celebrated with a victory ad. The management continued support of "the boys from Dayton's in the service," sending them letters of gratitude along with $10 American Express checks and assuring them they could work again at Dayton's if they chose. In the year following, the store developed for those at home a program for all its workers akin to today's employee assistance programs.

Constantly working towards their unspoken but driving intent to surpass Donaldson's and make Dayton's the largest local department store in sales, Nelson and Draper concentrated on customer services, anything to make the customers prefer buying at Dayton's. By 1919, for example, many single-horse- and team-drawn wagons painted with the store logo were transporting goods to customers' homes in some parts of town. In summer, a boat marked with the Dayton's logo met delivery wagons at Lake Minnetonka to take goods to resort patrons and lake residents. In winter, the horses pulled Dayton wagon bodies set on sleigh runners. After the war, Dayton's developed a full delivery system capable of handling "1,000 carpet-sweepers and 1,000 potted palms" a day. Automobiles were making an appearance, but horse-drawn vehicles carried heavy freight for another decade or longer.

What about airplanes? Just a decade after the store had displayed the Curtiss airplane, George devised another publicity stunt involving aviation, and so the *Journal* trumpeted in September 1919: "Flying Boat to Deliver Purchases." The store had offered free plane delivery for goods ordered by out-of town visitors at the Minnesota State Fair. In the end the scheme involved three Curtiss pilots and two mechanics in one trip by "flying boat" and three by airplane to 18 destinations northwest of Minneapolis. Later, during a freight embargo, the store gained publicity by flying in imported goods from New York—at high cost but bringing inestimable publicity to the store.

Shortly after Dayton's flying deliveries, Donaldson's captured attention with its million-dollar construction plan for an entirely new build-

Horse-drawn wagons delivered goods to Dayton's customers—and in summer, a boat took over at Lake Minnetonka.

ing. Crowded for space and looking to the future, Dayton's continued with its own long-range plan, in April 1920 starting a seven-story addition to the three-story section built four years earlier. Nelson contributed to all the construction plans, negotiations, and carry-through.

Poised for a new decade with good policy and programs, a fine physical plant, quality merchandise, well-trained, loyal personnel, and a reputation for innovative service, Dayton's had every reason to expect a profitable future, perhaps even to achieve its ever-more-burning desire to surpass Donaldson's. But the fear that prices would fall after the war materialized in the fall of 1920, when small banks around the country started to fail. Falling prices were inevitable.

The Dayton brothers in November ordered a temporary stop to buying new stock, a program of quick sales into February, and preparation of the staff for lower prices in the long term. Later, their father, George, remembered with store employees how the store got through this financial crisis: "The Dayton Company owed the banks $800,000. We told you to quit buying and to sell our merchandise and get ready for lower prices. Some of you recall the order issued in November 1920 that not a dollar of merchandise could be ordered by mail or telegraph, unless [Draper] signed it. We crowded sales and by February 5 we had paid the banks every dollar we owed them."

The store took huge markdowns, clearing itself of old inventory at market value so as to bring in fresh merchandise at lower cost. While taking a $675,000 loss covered by the reserve fund set up in 1914, the store paid off its debt, thus putting itself in a good financial position for sales over the long term. With its competitor Donaldson's holding onto older, more expensive merchandise and its old high prices, Dayton's was uniquely situated to outstock, outsell, and ultimately overtake Donaldson's as the city's leading department store. It proceeded to do just that, through two big sales.

In the first month of 1922, the store celebrated its 20th anniversary with a history of the store printed in the *Daytonews*, a large ad

Nelson Dayton in a rare photo of him during this period, with sons Donald and Bruce, ca. 1919

expressing appreciation to the citizens of Minneapolis, and its annual anniversary sale. The two-page history included a drawing of the original storefront (with a sign that said Dayton's, not Goodfellow's) as well as the current Dayton's complex. The ad praised both employees and customers.

Then, celebrating its 50th seasonal "old-fashioned bargain days" in October 1922, the store announced its intent to achieve the best sales day ever on Wednesday, October 11, through a sale dubbed *Jubilee!* It ordered double quantities of new goods, slashed prices to bring in new and ever-more-loyal customers, and heavily promoted the sale.

The crowd was the largest that the store had seen, and the sale was such a success that Dayton's executives, in New York at the time, wired for confirmation of the figures because they simply could not believe their eyes, The *Daytonews* later reported that the sale went "far over every quota, every previous figure, every expectation." Indeed it had—and with it Draper and Nelson reached their goal of pushing Donaldson's, which was still selling goods at wartime prices, out of the leading position. Dayton's was now the number-one department store in Minneapolis—and it held an annual *Jubilee!* through the rest of its long life.

Along with the pictures of his father, brother, and five sons, two short quotes long occupied a place of prominence on the wall behind Nelson's desk, each a reminder of his common sense and business philosophy. One read: "Always take a loss when there is a possibility

Dayton's candy kitchen, ca. 1920s

of a loss, and never take a profit until it is realized." The other: "A donkey can turn his back on his work, but a man has to face it." The wisdom of those quotes had led Dayton's to face up to its losses after the Great War and to take its place as the foremost department store of the area.

Given the effect of the war on U.S. business, the Daytons recognized that the world was getting smaller, and Nelson had a hand in making it more so. In the spring of 1922, the store's management—drawn by his enthusiasm for the idea—decided to look into radio as an advertising technique. Wanting more than commercials, Nelson meant for Dayton's to own, operate, and provide free programming on its own radio station, and so he moved a battery station to the second-floor radio department, put up an 80-foot aerial, and began broadcasting live piano music on May 11, 1922. In the weeks following, other local artists provided entertainment.

While from the beginning listeners marveled at the free entertainment, Nelson regretted that the station hyped as the most powerful in the Northwest did not reach as far as expected. The technology was still new, and even his advisors had not known that increasing wattage five times over the highest-powered station would not increase its power by five. Neither was the quality of sound what he wished. Believing the problems could be overcome, Nelson announced, "We won't quit while we're licked," closed the station temporarily, and set about rebuilding WBAH from the bottom up.

The reopened, Class B-licensed WBAH set broadcasting distance records first in the United States, then reached into Mexico and Alaska, and even to England and Germany. Before WBAH signed off two years later—donating its equipment to the nearby Dunwoody Institute—it provided entertainment including music, farm talks, and religious programs, as well as shows about Boy Scout work and fishing lore, and helped maintain communication with other cities during storms. Three months after it went off the air, 50 listeners in the United States and Canada had written to say how they had enjoyed tuning into "Willy Bah," as the station had come to be known.

Sometime in 1922, Nelson and Draper, who had for a time had made known their wish to acquire the one-twelfth shares of the business owned by each of their two sisters, were able to do so. Nelson wrote later:

> Finally Father came to us and said if we would give each of the girls $150,000 of The Dayton Company preferred stock for their $25,0000 of common stock and if we would agree to pay the girls 8 percent on that $150,000 of preferred stock . . . for a period of ten years, he would advise them to make the trade. Draper immediately objected to the proposition, saying that was altogether too much to pay them for their common stock.
>
> I [Nelson] . . . finally talked him into accepting Father's proposition. I knew Father would never give us another chance. Draper made one provision, however, and that was that if either he or I died, the survivor would not have to continue paying 8 percent if . . . we were up to date on paying the 8 percent. We made the deal and paid the girls 4 percent in February 1923.

Also that month, Nelson Dayton, who had given notes to his father—first for Oak Leaf Farm, then for his third of the store, and again for the lot and house on Blaisdell Avenue—celebrated the retirement of all his debt. He had become a successful merchant in his own right, and the business he owned mostly with his brother was thriving. There was nowhere to look but up.

In 1927, Nelson Dayton made the first telephone call ever between Minneapolis and London, from the Dayton store.

4

Master Manager

On a Monday evening in July 1923, Nelson's brother, Draper, fell ill after playing golf and returned to his summer home in Minnetonka with what appeared to be a stomach problem. His condition declined steadily until two days later, when on Wednesday, July 25, Draper died of heart failure at the age of 43.

The Dayton family was devastated. The store's employees and the citizens of Minneapolis were in shock when they read the next day the long, front-page newspaper articles about Draper, both general merchandising manager and general manager of Dayton's. Competing retailers ran ads of mourning. The Dayton Company announced the store would close for Draper's funeral on Friday.

Shattered by the loss of his son, George wrote immediately to daughter Josephine, in California, of Draper's death: "Nelson realizes the situation keenly—says quietly, 'I will be [general manager] and see what I can do.' Just how we shall plan in other ways we do not know."

Draper Dayton

On the Wednesday following Draper's funeral, George, who did not want to go on with the store, nevertheless spoke to employees in a positive vein:

> [Draper] loved this store; he loved his work; he loved the business; he loved to plan for it; he loved to see it grow . . .
>
> Nelson and I need your help, your cooperation, your assistance . . . I am going to resign some of the activities I have been connected with outside . . . and Nelson is going to take on other of Draper's responsibilities. But we cannot do it all, for I have sometimes said Draper was equal to five men. You will help, we know.

Sick at heart, George wanted to sell the store. But Nelson, who upon Draper's death essentially owned control of the company, wished to continue. He wrote later to his son Kenneth of the agreement he and his brother had made:

> Draper and I each put in provisions in our will that if [either brother] died, [his] common stock must be sold. When Draper died, my father and I had the right to buy the stock. Father wanted to sell the store out at that time, as he thought we couldn't run it, and said he didn't want to buy any of [Draper's] stock.
>
> I told him we would not sell, that we were going to run it for two or three years and . . . if we couldn't run it, we would sell before we ruined it, but I wanted to try.

Nelson, in recalling those days to his sons, said he hoped to be smart enough to sell it before it was ruined, but that he simply had to try to make a go of it. Reluctantly, George agreed, then advised Nelson regarding the purchase of Draper's third of the stock. Nelson recalled:

> I could have bought [Draper's] common stock at $68 a share under fair interpretation of our agreement. After his death, we found folded up with his will a sheet of paper with a lot of figures on it, in which he had used the figure $68 in figuring the value of his estate and how it would be divided under his will.
>
> Father took the position that the stock was worth more than $68, and I finally bought the stock at $80 a share . . . I accepted this higher value per share because I didn't want Draper's family to feel I had bought the stock too [cheaply].

With control of the vast majority of the common stock, Nelson chose, while providing limited stock options to some executives, to continue paying the 8 percent dividends to Josephine and Caroline. Nelson continued in his letter to Ken:

> Draper's death eliminated the necessity of paying the girls the extra dividend. Shortly after I got hold of Draper's stock, which gave me ten-twelfths of the store's common stock, or almost control, I sold small blocks to [store executives] Per-Lee, Larson, Arthur, and Luker. I told them that we were under no legal necessity to pay the extra payments on the preferred stock held by the girls.

But I told them I would not sell them common stock unless they signed an agreement that, if we were able . . . we would continue the extra payments as per the contract. They all agreed to this, and we continued the extra payments for the remaining nine and one-half years. This meant that each of the girls got some $70,000 extra dividend [that] we were not obligated to pay them.

The larger Dayton family in 1923, not long after Draper's death: (front row, l-r) G. Nelson Dayton holding Kenneth N. Dayton, David Dayton Blair, David Draper Dayton Jr., Bruce B. Dayton, Wallace C. Dayton, and Leonard V. Dayton; (second row) Donald C. Dayton, Bonney Blair (later Richardson), Helen Louise Hayden (later Chase), Dorothy Dayton (later Beck), William Frederick Hayden, and Josephine Dayton Blair holding Frederick Draper Blair; (third row) Grace Bliss Dayton, Ward W. Dayton, Louise Winchell Dayton (later Denman), and Avis Louise Dayton (later Heneman); (back) Caroline Dayton Hayden, George D. Dayton II, George D. Dayton, and Emma Chadwick Dayton.

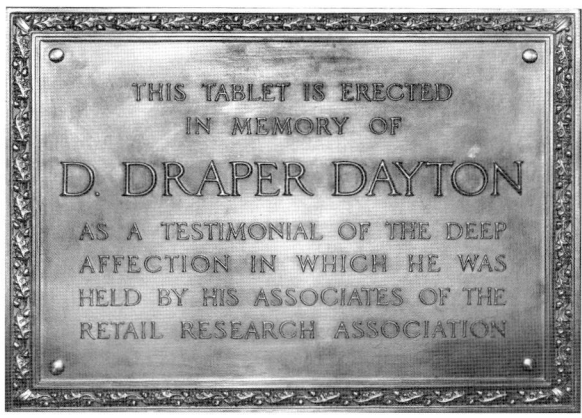

A bronze tablet memorializing Draper was erected at the store soon after his death in 1923.

Nelson paid Draper's estate for his common stock with "a big block of Dayton Company preferred stock and $390,000 in cash." Later writing to his son Bruce, Nelson noted that for the transactions involved he ultimately borrowed "between $600,000 and $700,000 from the Northwestern National Bank" and that he did not get out of debt again until 1942. He considered his debt an incentive as much as a burden, however, which strengthened his determination to see the store grow and thrive.

Given Nelson's decision to go ahead with the store, George rallied, and by September 1923 he was again showing some interest in its operation. He did not manage Dayton's, but Nelson gave him the title of president, and George served as the store's spokesperson. Nelson paid George an annual salary of $75,000, the same Nelson paid himself.

For his part, George also maintained his relationship with store employees, speaking with them as a group on many occasions, explaining store policy, providing background, noting economic trends, and generally providing context for the world of Dayton's.

A recurring theme was the company's bylaw stating that there must "never be any Sunday advertising by or in behalf of said compa-

Store window displays, 1923

ny" and the policy of "no Sunday work in this house," not even travel. "We have no Sunday traveling, except in this sense, that we have consented when some of you have been abroad and in the eastern cities and could not leave before, that you return early on Sunday morning so that you could be with your families," George said. Neither did the store light its street-level, holiday-display store windows on Sundays.

Nelson greatly missed Draper, but he accepted the loss and moved forward—ever grateful his brother had lived to see Dayton's surpass Donaldson's to become the leading department store in Minneapolis. That accomplishment was Nelson and Draper's shared legacy and Nelson's standard for further achievement in the store.

W. A. Dillman, A. C. White, and Alan Phillips

With the death of the store's dynamic leader and two other top executives who died earlier in the year, Nelson saw The Dayton Company's management as extremely weak. He resolved to build a strong team, vowing that the store would never become vulnerable in its management again. He took on the tasks and title of general manager (he considered that down-to-earth and descriptive title the best in the business) and brought others to the executive team through promotion and new hiring.

Nelson had helped in hiring controller W. A. Dillman to replace Ray Arnold in January 1923, as well in hiring A. C. White as superin-

John Per-Lee, C. J. Larson, and Hugh Arthur, shown later in life, were the first directors outside the Dayton family.

tendent and Alan Phillips as a divisional merchandise manager. Now he scoured the country for a general merchandise manager, finally selecting C. J. Larson, merchandise manager of The Downstairs Store. This proved a particularly happy choice. Nelson also elevated John A. Per-Lee to the position of assistant general manager, Hugh Arthur to publicity director, and John Luker to vice president and divisional merchandise manager.

In a move to broaden governance, Nelson named three of these men—John Per-Lee, C. J. Larson, and Hugh Arthur—to directorships in The Dayton Company, the first ones outside the Dayton family. Each bought 750 shares of the firm, with Nelson extending to them the same interest rate—2.5 percent—that the bank had given him. One new director, assuming that Nelson would sit at the head of the the board room table, sat at the other end. To his surprise, Nelson always sat in the middle.

Not much later, Nelson decided that two men employed elsewhere downtown would strengthen his team. The Minneapolis Retailers Association had agreed that its members would not hire from each other, but eventually both of these men—personnel director W. E. (Roy) Parmeter and merchandise manager David Birkett—joined the Dayton's coterie.

Every member of the team translated Nelson's program of building volume and goodwill into his own branch of management. Nelson's confidence in and respect for these men, his ability to give someone a job and then let him do it, is probably what freed him to say on occasion: "It is wise to put all your eggs in one basket—if you then watch the basket."

One day early in his tenure, Nelson walked by the reading room at the Minneapolis Club after lunch and spotted L. S. Donaldson, his chief merchandising competitor, having a conversation with Joe Chapman, a Northwestern National Bank executive. Nelson quietly took a nearby chair and, raising a newspaper to his face, eavesdropped on the conversation. He heard Donaldson offer Chapman—whose talents Nelson had, as a director of Northwestern, come to respect highly—the position of general manager at Donaldson's. Chapman later accepted.

Nelson had no reason to worry. He had put together a strong team, and with it he refined the Dayton Department Store's philosophy of serving a broad spectrum of the public, emphasizing these strategies for success:

- Capture the customers' imaginations with an array of goods.
- Earn loyalty with a generous merchandising policy (the root of Dayton's popular "returns" policy).
- Provide incidental attractions and conveniences within Dayton's walls so customers do not wander to the doors of competitors.

With these principles, Nelson and his team took Dayton's to three times the size of Donaldson's, earning a profit every year and, even during the Great Depression, paying undiminished dividends without fail.

Once Caroline Dayton Hayden, one recipient of the 8 percent dividends, teased her younger brother: "Nelson, everything's been handed to you on a silver platter."

Christmas shoppers thronged the sidewalk outside Dayton's, 1923.

Nelson agreed: "That's right, Caroline. And damn lucky for you I didn't spill it!"

More than that, Nelson supplied the energy, along with other "traits and talents," as C. J. Larson once wrote, "of incalculable value—great executive capacity, a cool head, and steady nerves." That Nelson had already earned the respect and confidence of the men and women around him was to the store's great advantage. He was decisive but laced his decisions with wit and goodwill in carrying the store forward.

In 1924, Dayton's said good-bye to its competitor L. S. Donaldson in an ad mourning his death at age 68. Donaldson's store nevertheless was Dayton's chief business rival: Through the year, local newspapers regularly reported on the "new glass block" kitty-corner from Dayton's.

Nelson's response continually gave voice to the principle of being all things to all people: "There is no reason . . . we should let any woman escape us to go to Chicago for her shopping."

In fact, he proposed to dominate retail within a 400-mile radius of Minneapolis. That meant broadening services whenever possible. In 1924, for example, the store established the "Sub-Deb Shop" to bring in teenage girls. The next year, 1925, The Dayton Company Studio made its debut; there the discriminating customer could find the latest thing in interior decoration.

Meanwhile, the Downstairs Store attracted those operating on more limited budgets. Dayton's also took over during that time the City of Minneapolis function of annually producing a Christmas play for children. And in 1926, a Dayton designer decided that if mechanical animals were good, live ones were better. With animals provided by "Fish" Jones of the city's Longfellow Gardens, the display made history in the retail world.

Nelson showed his mettle in deciding, when the term of the one remaining leased department ended, to keep women customers inside the store with an all-new beauty shop. The convenient and glamorous Looking Glass Salon soon became a Dayton's institution. Always receptive to innovation, Nelson introduced another service in 1927, choosing Marie Thompson Hill to be the store's first "stylist," who subsequently earned the store's reputation for a forward-looking fashion agenda. She brought in clothing designed by Lucien Lelong, for example, to sell in Dayton's French Room, which evolved first into the Model Room and then to the Oval Room.

Nelson's character and temperament made him an ideal instructor for the younger men of the store, primarily through example. They admired him as a "good gambler," someone who put resources on the line in support of thought-out decisions. C. J. Larson called it Nelson's "cool nerve," the poised control with which he supported promising projects and people. Convinced of a project's potential, he might authorize a budget of a quarter of a million dollars for one department alone. "That's a lot of money," Nelson said. "Spend it wisely." Once he placed faith in junior executives, he did not quibble or second-guess their decisions.

Young people in training also admired Nelson's determination to keep his staff content. His principle of building morale, even in harsh economic conditions, was simple and personal. He created an atmosphere of confidence, telling new management hires: "This is a job Dayton's needs to have done. I hope you're the [one] to do it. If not, I'll have to get one who can." He allowed his executives to grow in responsibility with the business, just as he encouraged the buyers to grow in taste with the times.

Nelson at his desk

Nelson used rebuke sparingly and with recognition of what was done well. "Never bawl a man out," he said, "except on company time. Don't do it at night or just before the weekend, when he'll have nothing to do but brood. If it has to be done, do it in the morning, when he can take out his reaction in work."

Once when the store hit a slump after a big *Jubilee!* sale, Nelson told executives, "The trouble is that you've done too well. You're getting complacent, and that's the worst sin in storekeeping."

Many associates admired Nelson most for his capacity for self-development. "He grew steadily in stature every year of his life," said one colleague.

Nelson was a faithful attender of RRA meetings, and he took to heart the tips his father passed on about department stores he saw in his travels. On March 3, 1925, for example, George wrote Nelson from Pasadena, California: "We went over yesterday to May & Co.'s opening. Crowds were there. Escalators, packed solid, worked perfectly—basement to 4th floor. Money has been spent freely to put building in condition for large volume."

The next day, George wrote:

> I had a very pleasant chat with Mr. Simon last evening. He says the clothing exceeds the furnishings—suits average $50 to $51, more under $35 upstairs—$21 in basement. I asked how they cleaned up, carrying such an immense stock—"by watching and training the salesmen."
>
> He says, "You can do an immense furnishings business . . . Get a good man who knows mdse.—that is the important thing."

Whether on his father's advice or his own good counsel, Nelson eventually added men's furnishings to Dayton's offerings. His timing was right, the customers approved, and the store's bottom line went up.

The same month, George made a comment pertinent in the light of Nelson's also having, with Grace, produced five sons: "Introduced myself to Mr. Gimbel of New York . . . He says secret of their success was there were five brothers—different—and they pulled together. Now have five stores, as you know."

Four days later, George complimented Nelson on his operation of Dayton's: "I am quite impressed by the smaller amount of [bills payable] as we get the comparisons now. It looks like better merchandising . . . Surprised we cashed more checks than [Donaldson's] . . . Wish we could learn how the banks treat them."

Both Nelson and George shared their views of the industry with employees in the company newsletter, *Daytonews*. In the September 1925 issue, for example, appeared the reiteration of a conversation with department managers on one of Nelson's favorite themes:

> Successful businessmen are much more concerned about the way their business will be run when they are no longer at the helm than in personally making money. The only real insurance we can provide is by developing a corps of younger men who are potential executives . . . Only as we actually put the load on the shoulders of our younger men [can we] fit them for responsibilities.
>
> . . . There is ample room for all of you, and more, if only you will keep growing . . . Nowhere in the U.S. is there a greater chance than in this store.

In a February 1926 letter from California, George rejoiced in The Dayton Company's current balance sheet, wishing to study "comparative figures for the RRA [Retail Research Association]." Then, after a discussion of what Congress might do with corporate tax rates and how much the store should set aside, he noted: "Gratification grows with contemplation. Now, we can properly study how to improve service and . . . spend some money to . . . get our service on best possible sensible basics."

By this time almost 70 years of age, George continued to express pleasure in good news and to offer advice and encouragement on an almost daily basis. On March 9, 1926, he wrote Nelson about a comparative report on store personnel, delighted that "Dayton's stands so high with college graduates."

On March 17, 1926, George referred to the new clothing department for men that Dayton's opened in 1926, and later that month he wrote of some potential competition: "I don't suppose Joe [Chapman, general manager of Donaldson's], or we, can do much, but if any of us can exercise any influence I think we ought to get Sears Roebuck inside of St. Paul almost anywhere in preference to [Minneapolis]." Sears ended up building its tower in Minneapolis—but on Lake Street, not downtown.

George's final 1926 letter from California described his meetings with two retailers there, the first of whom offered to buy out Dayton's. George's response showed that, due to Nelson's good management, he clearly was in favor of keeping the store:

Dayton's men's department, 1926

Mr. May said he figured at one time on getting Donaldson's—they would be glad to get another store—then asked, "How would you like to sell out?"

"We desire to be active and prefer to keep rather than sell," [I answered].

"You can stay with us. We would be glad to have you and your son go right on with us."

. . . I was glad to have the conversation abruptly stopped, but I remarked, "There are nine Dayton boys [including cousins] coming on."

Nelson heard similar offers during the years 1927–1929, when *consolidation* was the buzzword of American retail, and many of the larger department store chains were formed. Allied Stores Corporation acquired L. S. Donaldson of Minneapolis, for example, in 1928, continuing to operate that store under its original name.

Investment bankers, eyeing the opportunity Dayton's might represent for them, frequently called on Nelson Dayton, who with five sons had no intention of selling the region's leading department store. He entertained their offers with tongue-in-cheek agreement and his own provisos: "Well, I'd have to take down the name," or "I'd have to depart from the management," he kidded them, knowing full well that they coveted the name *Dayton's* as well as its reputation and the talents of its general manager.

In the meantime, George was sending Nelson gentle warnings: "May and Bullock think mdse. is going to be somewhat cheaper and are inclined to go slow on future buying," backing his prediction—in 1926—that economic depression was on the way. Despite George's prescience, or perhaps because The Dayton Company wished to expand while it could, Nelson and most of the store's managers were planning for the opening of a branch store on the University of Minnesota campus the next year.

The store had arranged for broadcast over radio station WCCO an ambitious program of six, monthly, privately sponsored concerts,

Dayton's University Store, 1930

starting on Thanksgiving 1927, the year Dayton's and the Minneapolis Symphony Orchestra celebrated their 25th anniversaries. Nelson believed radio was important in light of the store's rule against advertising in Sunday newspapers. Direct mail helped, and radio did the rest.

Nelson translated the store's penchant for honesty in advertising into common sense. With little taste for extravagance, he said, "Only one thing can be superlative at one time." Exaggeration destroyed the

One of the Dayton's University Store's two restaurants, in 1934

meaning of words, not to mention customer confidence. "How very much better for the customer to be surprised," he said, "when she discovers how great the bargain really is. When she tells her friends . . . that is worth a lot more to us than any claim we could invent."

Further, he noted, "We don't want customers to keep merchandise with which they are not entirely satisfied. If we allow credits with a smile and a 'Thank You,' that is the best kind of advertising we can get. And it is free."

The radio program was just one part of the celebration of Dayton's 25th anniversary. Before the Silver Anniversary Sale, the store offered to pay 15 cents apiece for dimes, 35 cents for quarters, 65 cents for half-dollars, and $1.25 for dollars minted in 1902, the year the store had opened. On February 5, 1927, right before he left for Pasadena,

George wrote his grandson, Draper's son George (at Princeton), about the result: "The 43,022 pieces [valued at $12,605 U.S.] were put in the window at the corner of 7th and Nicollet; a guard outside and one inside was kept night and day to protect them during the 54 hours the silver was there. Of course, it attracted a great deal of attention and created a great deal of talk all over town."

The other 21 stores of the AMC had offered congratulations by means of advertisements in Minneapolis newspapers on the big day. Several of the ads—those of Strawbridge and Clothier of Philadelphia and B. Forman of Rochester, New York, for example—mentioned that their own executives occasionally visited Dayton's in Minneapolis "to study [its] innovations and improvements in storekeeping." Just one example of the store's leading edge was Nelson's historic telephone call, the first one made between Minneapolis and London. A picture of him conversing with a representative of the store's buying office in London (see chapter opening) resulted in more great publicity.

Around that time, Dayton's learned that in a count made by a firm interested in locating in Minneapolis, some 12,000 people passed the Dayton's corner at Seventh and Nicollet in the same time 9,000 people passed the Donaldson's corner at Nicollet and Sixth. The figures upheld George's earlier claim that Nicollet and Seventh Street comprised the city's "100 percent corner." That year, when one of his favorite charities, the YWCA, erected a new, eight-story facility on the northwest corner of 12th and Nicollet, kitty-corner from Westminster Presbyterian Church, George predicted that the downtown would never "jump" those nonprofit barriers to the south. Both of his predictions proved accurate: In contrast to the instability of the downtowns of other cities, Minneapolis's prime commercial downtown still lies north of 12th Street. And Seventh and Nicollet remains the "100 percent" corner.

Determined to make its 26th year even better than the 25th, Dayton's in 1928 offered extra cash for 1902 coins, this time adding nickels to the cache. Its anniversary sale ad concluded, however, that

Above: Construction for the 1928 parking garage addition
Below: The finished project on Eighth Street

bargains counted more: "The proof of the pudding is in the eating, whether it be served in a *silver* dish or in some other."

Dayton's soon announced another innovation—a parking garage for its customers. *Minneapolis Journal* headlines proclaimed: "Wrecking Starts for New Dayton 4-Story Garage. Company Acquires Lease on 50-Foot Plot Adjoining the Eighth Street Property. Building to Care for 300 Autos." On September 1, 1928, the garage, plus its basement expanding the Downstairs Store and its sub-basement providing more room for delivery, made its debut. The opening brought the area of the total Dayton's facility to "17 acres," or 740,520 square feet.

On December 17, 1928, The Dayton Company celebrated the 50th wedding anniversary of the elder Daytons—at the store: "Before 10:00 A.M. 2,300 employees of The Dayton Company shook hands with Emma and George on the fourth floor of the store, and each guest received a small souvenir box containing a piece of fruit cake."

Then, on January 16, 1929, reported the *Daytonews:* "Eleven hundred Daytonians flocked to the tea rooms . . . to pay honor to Mr. and Mrs. George D. Dayton at the Golden Wedding party . . . We saw rows of tables, each with its own centerpiece of golden daffodils . . . yellow community song sheets at each place. [Emma's] place was marked with a lovely corsage."

Emma died three years later, and George hadn't the heart even to attend the annual store Christmas party without her. His concern for details of the business dwindled, but he noted in a public letter to high-school graduates: "This store has become the largest west of Chicago and east of California."

In the summer of 1929 The Dayton Company purchased the reputable J. B. Hudson Company (now JB Jewelers). Nelson named George president (again George served as spokesman but played no part in management) of the jewelry retailing concern, and George announced plans to construct an elegant store on the corner of Nicollet and Eighth, with egress to and from the department store.

George and Emma Dayton celebrated their 50th wedding anniversary on January 16, 1929.

Almost immediately the stock market plummeted, and the Great Depression began. With wry humor, Nelson later advised his sons never to buy a jewelry store just before a market crash.

Still, in 1930, the store had the biggest year in its history to date. And in the years of hard times that followed, The Dayton Company, under Nelson's management, made progress against its competition and continued to show a profit, though somewhat reduced.

George Dayton originated the store's first reserves, but Nelson carried through on the idea that thrift during prosperity buys advantage during adversity. He advised buyers to get the longest terms possible for payment of goods. On contracts calling for six or nine months' settlement, they could anticipate the deadlines for payment. The store's healthy reserves enabled it to pay such bills "early" and thus deduct the 6 percent interest otherwise payable from the amount due its creditors. The store passed on part of such savings in its lower prices to customers while adding the remainder to its capital reserve bond fund for expansion.

This kind of practice was especially important to Dayton's during hard times, and in 1932 the store tried a variation on this theme. The full effect of the economic depression was just beginning to reach what was still then called "the Northwest," and Nelson was determined to hold it off if he could. He had C. J. Larson tell the manager of the men's department: "The general manager has selected a certain number of departments for an experiment in getting volume. Yours is one. Concentrate on just one item."

The buyer promptly said, "Overcoats," and went to Ohio to purchase an entire carload—1,164 coats. The order made history in the small manufacturing town and won headlines in Minneapolis papers. The number of coats sold on the first day made the sale one of the store's most successful ever. Without healthy reserves, Dayton's would not have been able to order or pay for those coats.

Dayton's window display of women's fashion, 1930. Note the Woodhill Country Club (Minnetonka) setting.

Despite the economic depression, 1930 was Dayton's biggest year to date.

Nelson's philosophy of retail became with the depression ever more imaginative and exploratory. One great sale followed another. The Downstairs Store instituted Early Bird sales and a Red Arrow Booth to which customers arrived by following arrows painted on the floor. Storewide sales went on as usual: Old-Fashioned Bargain Days and inventory sales were preludes to the traditional Daisy and *Jubilee!* sales.

Dayton's ability to buy in great quantity was also evident at the Bigger Business Day of April 18, 1932, when the store offered 180,000 pairs of silk stockings—of chiffon or service weight—at two pairs for $1, as well as 15,000 men's broadcloth shirts at 59 cents each. Such sales increased Dayton's volume, brought costumers downtown, and helped maintain supplier output during the Great Depression. In addition the sales provided work for as many as 1,000 extra salespeople at Dayton's in a single day.

Still, profits were dwindling, and in 1932, the store's worst year, Dayton's made only $436,249, or 38 percent of the profits it had made in 1929 ($1,144,022). (See chart on pages 206–207.) Some departments—for example, those selling "luxury" goods—simply weren't making it. The manager of the Oriental rug department asked, "Are you going to cut my salary?" And Nelson answered, "Well, that's not on my agenda, but I'll be glad to discuss it with you." He was taking the larger view: Compared with the average 55 percent decrease in sales for department stores in the East, the store was doing well. He attributed at least part of Dayton's success to the relatively healthy economy of Minneapolis and the Northwest, but his good management accounted for much of it.

As the store's volume increased, Nelson kept pushing for more. "I'm not paid to be satisfied," he told associates. "If I thought you were satisfied, you wouldn't occupy the positions you do." Through it all, The Dayton Company paid its shareholders undiminished dividends.

The depression of the 1930s was hard on George. He and Emma had endowed their Dayton Foundation generously, and little remained of their income when the value of real estate fell. Nelson continued to pay George an annual salary equal to his own through those hard times.

George appreciated that, as well as the value of Nelson's advice. In writing Josephine about some recent financial arrangement, he noted:

> I am glad Nelson suggested this to me and hope it will prove helpful to Caroline and Josephine, and someday something be left for the grandchildren, who may then need it more than any of us need it now . . . Nelson has been very thoughtful in trying to plan for his father and each of his sisters in various ways, so that we all may be a little more comfortable if financial losses should come.

The high rate of unemployment was as evident in Minnesota as in the rest of the country. Nelson worked to keep as many people employed as he could. According to employee E. S. Larsen:

The office manager went to [Nelson] and told him that because of the low-volume trend . . . he could drop five sales-audit girls. Mr. Dayton shook his head negatively, so that settled that matter. Later he explained that some people would slash expenses by dropping people, when by so doing they merely added to the depression and created trouble and privations for those who lost their jobs. This was sound and farsighted thinking . . . typical of this man.

Nelson worked as hard as his father to make employees feel they were part of The Dayton Company family, practicing a kind of paternal supervision, also learned from George. Discipline was brisk, direct, and rooted in principle: "Don't tell me what we're good at," he said. "Tell me what we're poor at so that we can manage to do better." When they did that, he followed through with forward-thinking personnel benefits such as paid vacations, a shorter work week, insurance and educational programs, an employee lunch room, and planned social events.

Nelson took that attitude even when, in 1934, Minneapolis was the scene of a violent teamster demonstration. When the teamsters tried to unionize Dayton's truck drivers, he wrote this (undated) letter to employees:

> The loyalty and good work of those connected with the Dayton Company have indicated to us their faith in the efforts of the management to serve their interests, as well as those of the public and the owners. We cherish this loyalty.
>
> The Dayton Company has been fortunate from its beginning in having an unusually fine personnel. That, and Daytonians' loyalty and cooperation, have contributed largely to the development of the institution and to the corresponding increase in the number of its employees.
>
> It has been the aim of The Dayton Company management to promote from among our own people as far as possible. For years we have tried to fill from 75 percent to 80 percent of vacancies occurring in the store from our own staff; we do not think it wise to fill all va-

cancies from inside, since it is often advisable to bring in new blood with new ideas. Nearly all those now in important positions as department managers . . . assistants, or divisional merchandising managers, have grown up and developed with The Dayton Company.

We think the high standard of personnel we have been able to secure has been due in part to the favorable conditions of employment here and the belief of those employed here that they would receive fair play.

The Dayton Company is and has been willing to discuss with any one or any group in the store their hours of work, their salaries, and their working conditions. These may be discussed with Mr. A. C. White, Mr. W. E. Parmeter, or Mr. G. N. Dayton. We cannot imagine any matters or circumstances existing or arising which could not be adjusted to the best advantage of both you and the management, in frank, tolerant, and cooperative conference between ourselves.

Despite Nelson's efforts, the Dayton's drivers voted to and did unionize in 1934, though none of the store's other workers ever did. Nelson worked to maintain good relations with the drivers, just as he had in the past.

Nelson celebrated his silver anniversary of service with The Dayton Company in 1935, the November *Daytonews* of that year noting the occasion with a short article on his career with the store. In part it read: "We think of him as being on the job every day, as many hours as anyone; [as] keeping the door of his office always open; and as being frank, laconic, just, and sincere."

With all of Dayton's employees focused on increasing sales volume, a clamor for more space was inevitable. Previous expansion had taken Dayton's over the years to nine stories in one section, and ten in another. But in the mid-1930s, some divisions were still operating in structures only three stories high. These buildings stood at the corner of Nicollet and Eighth Street—the site of the 1917 fire and by this time of J. B. Hudson's—and were held by an out-of-town group with a 100-year lease. It was one of the last pieces under the store not owned by the Dayton Foundation or The Dayton Company. Nelson felt the time was right to acquire the property outright.

After negotiations lasting almost a year, the parties reached agreement on August 24, 1937, thanks to assistance to The Dayton Company by Thorpe Brothers, real estate dealers of Minneapolis. New England Mutual Life Insurance Company of Boston lent the store $1,500,000 to take full possession of the land. When Bill Huff, a good friend of Nelson's and the vice president of another local company, learned that Dayton's was able to borrow for real estate at 2.5 percent interest while Honeywell had to pay 2.625, he protested: "But you're not a better risk."

To this Nelson replied, "Well, here's where the figures tell."

After closing on that Eighth and Nicollet property, Nelson admitted that "retarding conditions" were adversely affecting business, but he said he expected these to change soon. Dayton's bought the land, he said, because "we are able to borrow the money necessary at a rate somewhat lower than the rate [of] the rental."

"We are quite willing," he concluded, "to have this purchase interpreted as an evidence of the faith of our preferred and common stockholders in the future of Minneapolis and the Northwest. Our business is owned entirely by residents of Minneapolis or members of their families, and almost entirely by persons actually engaged in conducting the store."

So with the Great Depression still casting its shadow, Nelson risked investment for the future—in land and new construction. Before the real estate deal was complete, he announced that improvements costing $1,000,000 would begin immediately. The section housing the garage was to reach 10 stories, with that over Hudson's reaching to 7 stories—further steps towards George's 12-story vision.

The added space would allow the expansion of several departments plus improvement of the garage and tea rooms and other services. Air-

Dayton's depression-era expansion included air-conditioned shopping areas. Note the lettering on the Nicollet (right) frontage.

conditioning of the old quarters and most of the new would "give our patrons in Minneapolis and Northwest as complete facilities for their shopping as are enjoyed in any city in this country."

On February 5, 1937, Nelson wrote his son Bruce, at Yale, updating him on the latest sale and on his progress towards paying off his personal debt:

> The second week of the Anniversary Sales has been good but not quite as good as we had hoped for. I presume it never will be.
>
> My note came due at the N. W. National Bank today. I paid off $35,000 on the principal and signed a new note for $100,000. I hope I can get that cleaned up in a couple of years . . . With the exception of about eight months in 1923, I have been in debt since

1907. I would have been out of debt by this time, but a year ago I borrowed $110,000 to buy $100,000 insurance [from] Prudential and an annuity [that] would pay me about $3,200 a year.

. . . One nightmare that I have always had [is] that I might go along pretty well until I [am] about 60 and then go busted and not be able to get in anywhere. Unless everything goes to the devil, I can count on this $3,200 a year and would not starve on that—so I have had a lot of satisfaction this past year with that annuity.

Nelson needn't have worried. Dayton's celebrated more than $17 million in sales in 1937, the year George celebrated his 80th birthday.

George had two years earlier given up his 16-block walk from home to the store with Nelson; after that George arrived at the store not so frequently and in a wheelchair. By 1937 in rapidly failing health and largely confined to his bedroom, he worked a few hours a day, putting his affairs in order. On February 18, 1938, George Draper Dayton died at his home at 2020 Blaisdell, content that Nelson had more than brought the store through difficult times—and that Nelson's oldest son, Donald, had entered the business.

In fact, Nelson had built on George's vision and beyond. The business covered many times the space it had upon its opening in 1902. The store employed many more than its initial 240 workers. Nelson had brought Dayton's through the Great Depression, making a profit every year, helping the city and region through hard times, broadening and deepening its role as a cultural force in Minneapolis, and making it a positive part of the lives of its patrons, employees, neighbor businesses, and the wider community.

And he would do more.

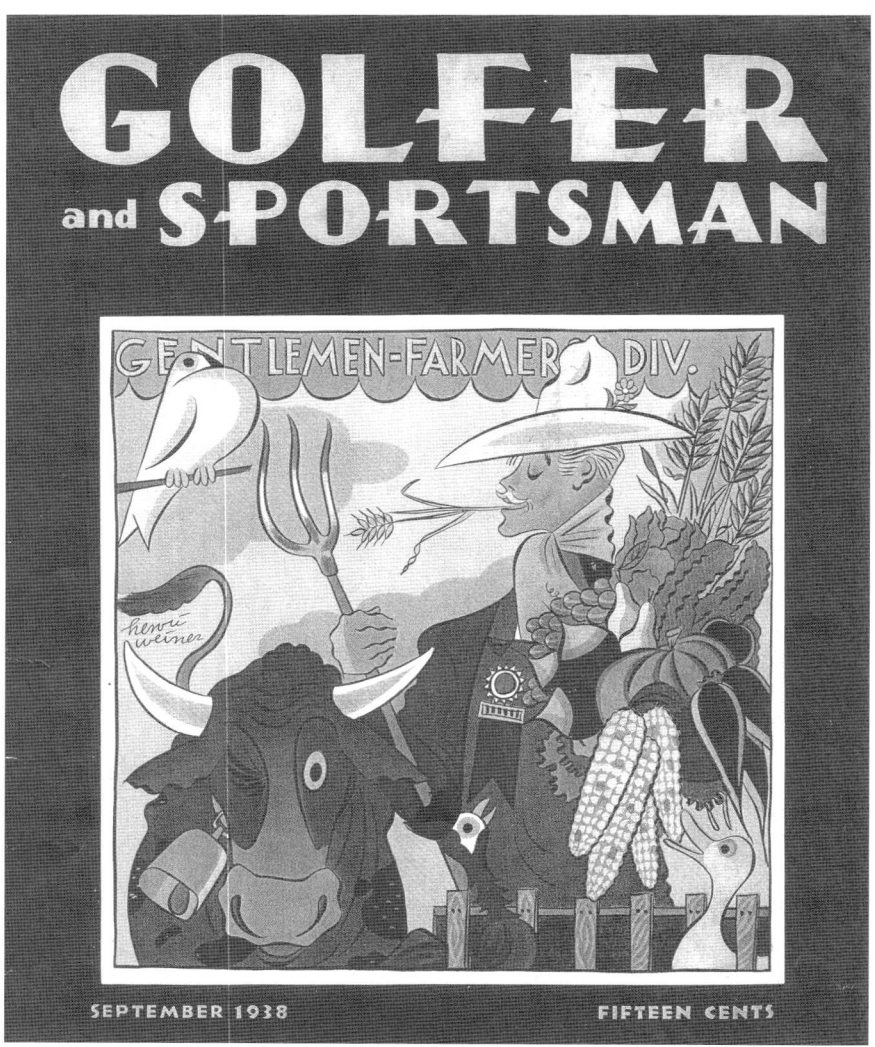

The September 1938 Golfer and Sportsman *featured Boulder Bridge Farm, which sported a sign at its entrance: "Visitors Invited Every Day except Sunday."*

# 5

Boulder Bridge Farm

Early in 1926, *Country Life* magazine ran an ad for the sale of Rose Farm—near Smithtown Bay off Lake Minnetonka, not far from the town of Excelsior. Nelson and Grace Dayton recognized it as perhaps the perfect place to rear their five sons and to satisfy Nelson's agricultural interests. They decided to take a look.

Edmund J. Longyear, an engineer holding the patent on a major innovation in drills for mining, had 18 years earlier bought the 90-acre farm fronting on 1,500 feet of lakeshore. He built there a home designed by Jackson M. Stone of J. M. Lyton Architects, Minneapolis. A maple woods covered the ridge just north of the house.

By the time the Daytons viewed the property, Longyear had drained the swamp at the bottom of the hill to create a sweep of lawn on the west shore, commissioned gardens, built a greenhouse and boathouse, and dredged the lagoon. A local mason, perhaps Norman Borlaug, had built a fieldstone bridge above the entrance to the lagoon, and others had crafted fieldstone walls and gate pillars at the farm's entrance. In 1915, Longyear added a 150-foot barn, accommodating 10 cows, four horses, and assorted machinery. Largely retired from engineering, Longyear became one of several "gentleman farmers" raising racehorses and cattle in the area.

The property, which had two water supplies—from the lake and a deep well—indeed had potential. The Daytons decided to buy the farm, and in a nod to the rearing of their five sons—Donald, Bruce, Wallace, Kenneth, and Douglas—they renamed Rose Farm for the bridge crossing the lagoon. Thus the start of Boulder Bridge Farm Company, as it was soon incorporated—where cows, horses, and boys thrived.

Nine Guernseys, some draft horses, and a few pigs were included in the purchase price of the farm. Adding over time to the farm's 90 acres to create a property of about 800 acres so as to keep livestock and feed production in balance, Nelson and Grace happily brought their sons to the country for the summers of their growing-up years. The Daytons picked the earliest possible spring date each year to shift their household from city to farm, taking pride in being the first on

Boulder Bridge Farm

The Boulder Bridge Farm family residence

the lake each spring (usually April 1) and the last to leave for the city in the fall.

Nelson intended to make more of Boulder Bridge than a gentleman's farm. He wanted to apply there the principles of scientific farming to a practical farming situation. In making the farm a leading breeder of Guernsey cattle and Belgian horses, he provided for his sons another example of doing "only what you can do as well as it can be done anywhere."

In fact, Nelson's cattle did so well—they won 218 championships and 590 blue ribbons in 24 years, including more Grand Championships (eight) at the National Dairy Show than any other exhibitor—that at the end of that period, half of all the Guernseys at the Minnesota State Fair had Boulder Bridge blood in their veins.

Nelson liked winning prizes, but his real aim was to improve and sell the Boulder Bridge livestock as a way to build the quality of the herds in Minnesota and other midwestern states. And he indicated

Les Wilson (above with Nelson and a prize Guernsey) was general superintendent of the farm.

the seriousness of his farming intentions almost immediately after the transfer of ownership by hiring Leslie (Les) V. Wilson, a progressive agriculturalist, to serve as general superintendent of the farm.

Wilson, a professor of dairy husbandry at the University of Minnesota, reportedly was "as practical as a pitchfork, as competitive as a race horse." His father had been a livestock commission merchant in the stockyards at Chicago. His uncle was "Tana Jim" Wilson, U.S. Secretary of Agriculture serving Presidents McKinley, Theodore Roosevelt, and Taft. After graduating from Iowa State College at Ames, Les Wilson was in charge of Minnesota's dairy extension work.

Nelson Dayton set out to modernize the farm and dairy facility as Wilson searched out the best hands and best breeding stock he could find. In short order, Wilson hired Olaf Kjome as head dairy herdsman and Dalt Long as head horseman. Both the Wilson and Kjome families (Wilson had three children and Kjome, five) lived at Boulder Bridge too.

Always more interested in breeding good stock than in buying it, Nelson instructed the purchase of only a few good bulls and stallions to start with, then took pride in raising bulls and cows, then stallions and mares, of superior quality.

Before bringing his family for its first season at Boulder Bridge, Nelson had the family residence rewired and plumbed. He gradually added barns and upgraded the old farmhouse, then built a new one, where 15 to 20 farm employees could live. Some of them were young men earning their way through or just out of ag school, hoping to make a career in the field. Two on-site cooks provided three meals for employees Monday through Saturday.

Nelson's mother, Emma, a frequent visitor to Boulder Bridge, counted places at the farmhouse table to determine how many peo-

Boulder Bridge Farm

Nelson and Grace named Boulder Bridge Farm for the bridge crossing the lagoon, a nod to their five sons: (l-r) Douglas, Bruce, Wallace, Kenneth, and Donald.

ple worked on the farm, but Nelson said, "You can't really tell from that." Beside those caring for livestock and raising their feed, the farm employed full-time gardeners and landscape workers. Every year, for example, they trimmed the buckthorn hedge along the roadside boundaries.

Chauffeur Vernon Benson also lived at the farm, in an apartment above the garage, when the Daytons were there. He drove the boys to school each day and served as Grace's driver when she had meetings in the city. Eventually, he taught all the boys to drive.

Grace ran the households in town and country with the help of Christine Thune (Ken called her "Toonie"), a young woman emigrated from Norway. She began working with the Daytons in 1926 and remained with the family 45 years. There was also a night watchman for the farm. Altogether, as many as 45 employees worked at Boulder Bridge at a time.

Grace looked forward to the family's annual spring-through-fall seasons at the farm, where she tended to the boys, the house, the greenhouse, and further developed the flower and vegetable gardens. There was already a formal garden between the family residence and the barns, with flowerbeds and walking paths. Grace added a shady rock garden outside the home's eating porch and a stream garden with wildflowers—trilliums and violets, maintained by a wildflower specialist. Grace loved and protected the wildflowers abundant in the maple woods as well. Three men helped her with Boulder Bridge gardening and landscaping on a regular basis.

Once, when Grace wanted some plantings along the boathouse stream south of the lagoon, Nelson said it would cost too much. She answered dryly, "About as much as two cows," to win her case. He asserted later that it turned out to be much more than that.

Nelson appreciated to a great degree the 78 species of trees he counted growing at Boulder Bridge Farm. He enjoyed being out of

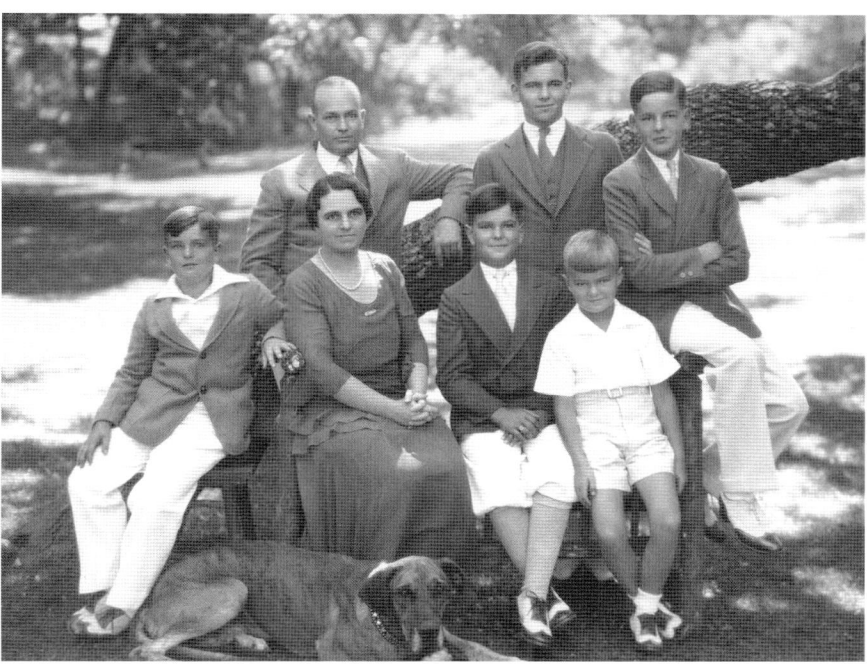

Back row (l-r): Nelson, Don, and Bruce; front: Ken, Grace, Wally, and Doug

*The Dayton boys (l-r, with Grace and their mascot Chum):
Don, Bruce, Wally, Ken, and Doug*

doors, and he personally cut brush on the farm for exercise, preferring to do that work alone.

The Dayton boys—Don was 12 years old, Bruce 8, Wally 5, Ken 4, and Doug 2 in their first summer at the farm—spent their mornings in the barns with their mascot, a Newfoundland named Chum. Once he was old enough, each brother worked for ten cents an hour in the cow or horse barns—each chose which he preferred.

Returning to the house for lunch, the boys swam or played in the afternoons. A local college student, Bill Deutsche, served as their companion through many summer days; another young man taught them how to swim. The boys also bicycled, rowed and sailed, fished and camped, and played tennis. In winter they enjoyed sledding and skiing on the grounds.

The two oldest boys each received a Welsh pony upon their first spring at the farm, and each had responsibility for grooming and feeding his mount. Donald's pony was named Pal, and Bruce's was Pet. Wally and Kenny, when they were old enough, had ponies Dusky and Daisy, which they often hitched to a lumber wagon. Don and Bruce liked to follow and "rob" them. After a few years, Doug, the youngest, also cared for his own pony.

All the riders in the family, led by Nelson and Grace, rode English saddle on trails around the farm almost every Saturday and Sunday. Nelson's favorite breed of riding horse was the Tennessee Walker. Grace loved to ride fast on her former polo pony, Lorraine, and the boys followed.

Given the boys' active life, they often displayed cuts and scrapes, not to mention the normal childhood diseases. Excelsior physician Hugh Arey made house calls at Boulder Bridge and once recommended poison-ivy sandwiches as a way to develop immunity to the plant. The boys described the "going in" as much better than the "coming out," however, and after the first round, that experiment was dropped.

Wally, Doug, and Ken in their lumber wagon, drawn by ponies Daisy and Dusky, ca. 1928

Nelson regretted that his own father had never taught him the facts of life and that he had had to learn about sex "in the gutter." He thought Boulder Bridge a good place to impart the knowledge of reproduction in a wholesome way to his sons at an appropriate young age. (Bruce once asked his father what "being in heat" meant). Nelson showed the brothers, one at a time, how the horses were bred. Once indoctrinated, each could watch the procedure whenever he wished.

The brothers did work appropriate to their age. One might muck out the stalls, another help with a younger animal, another with general chores. Doug recalled being "a driver's helper on the farm truck. Mostly what we hauled was manure, loaded and unloaded by hand. We had a wonderful bunch of farmers to work with; you worked right alongside them. You couldn't take advantage of your position." Along the way, all the brothers learned about dairying and about caring for and showing animals in the ring.

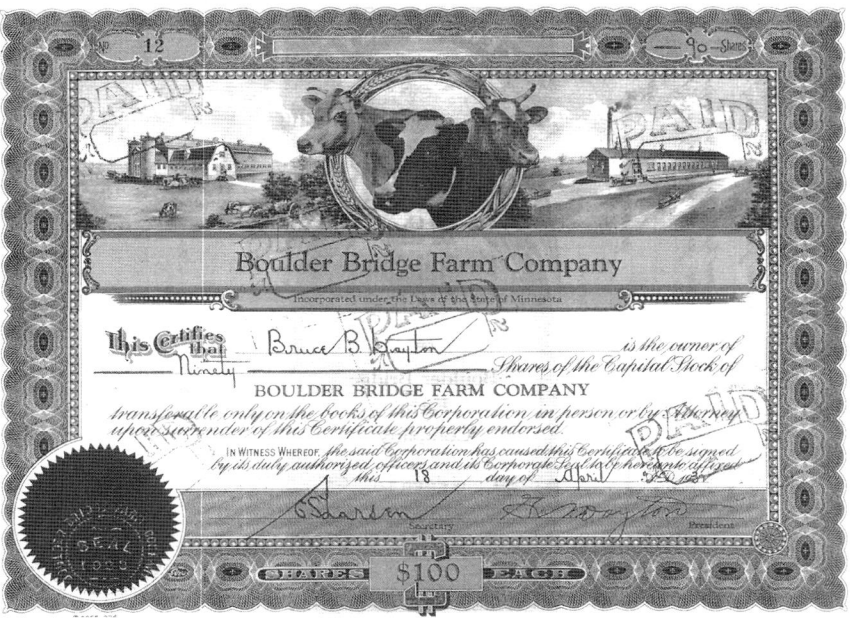

Nelson gave a share or two of Boulder Bridge Farm to each son.

Bruce with his Welsh pony, Pet

Donald, the oldest, was a cowman and the only brother to participate in 4-H. In 1927 a member of the Hennepin County 4-H Calf Club, he took honors for his effort with a dairy heifer, which included conditioning, showmanship, and the presentation of a well-researched report. The prize was a trip to the International Stock Show (Chicago) with 20 other boys from around the state.

Donald's brothers preferred to work in the horse barns. Bruce, the most proficient rider, was the only one to compete in the ring. At age 8 he won first prize in his first competition at the Woodhill Country Club horse show with his pony, Pet, pulling a cart. Later he competed in the equestrian class at the Minnesota State Fair, winning first prize in his first competition there too.

Each brother looked forward to riding in a freight car with Boulder Bridge livestock to state fairs in the region—Minnesota, Wisconsin, Illinois, Iowa, or Indiana. Doing so at about age 14 or 15 was a Dayton rite of passage.

The family ate meals together at Boulder Bridge, Nelson driving to and back from the downtown store to be home in time for dinner. Before he left each morning, he stopped by Superintendent Wilson's office, then used his driving time to the department store to think of names for newborn calves. The first year he chose names starting with the letter A—Alice, Anna, and Anita—and the second year he chose names starting with the letter B—Becky, Betsy, Barbara—and so on into the alphabet. That way he knew, just by the first letter of the name of the cow, which year she was born.

Nelson gave as long a rope to Superintendent Wilson as he did to the managers of Dayton's Department Store, and Wilson used it wisely. He believed, along with Nelson, that cows benefit from human contact, so most of them were milked by hand. Boulder Bridge residents, a few neighbors, and the patrons of Dayton's Tea Room, which bought most of the farm's milk, enjoyed the result.

Wilson wrote later that L. S. Page, president of the Page Hill Lumber Company and a longtime friend of Nelson, knew of his work with Guernseys and had recommended him. In the first year, the farm, under Wilson's supervision, purchased nine purebred Guernseys, more after expansion including a new cattle barn—and a horse barn to match.

The herd of dairy cows eventually grew to more than 225 animals. Over the life of the farm, more than 1,700 calves were registered with the American Guernsey Cattle Club, many of them sold, along with Nelson's young bulls, to farmers across the state. The Boulder Bridge herd—for its 24 years on continuous testing—averaged 433 pounds of butterfat per cow annually. (In light of emerging concerns about high cholesterol, Nelson might not today take such pride in the huge amounts of butterfat his herd produced.)

Residents of the farm, a few neighbors, and the patrons of Dayton's Tea Room enjoyed milk from the Boulder Bridge dairy herd. The Milk Counter, 1941, may have been set up for a special Dayton's event.

The Long Pull

In 1949, the year before dispersal, the herd of 90 to 100 milking cows produced more than 900,000 pounds of milk. According to Superintendent Wilson, all the surplus milk products, eggs, and poultry, including chickens and turkeys, went to The Dayton Company Tea Rooms.

Starting in 1935, Boulder Bridge Farm added some 600 acres to its holdings, and the farm from that time produced all its own feed other than wheat, bran, and linseed meal. As many as 28 horses in the harness at a time did most of the heavy work in the field. There was just one tractor, used for the jobs too impractical for horses to complete. The Belgians, most starting in the hitch at about three years of age, were housed in an immaculate stable with 10 box stalls and 20 tie stalls. More than 200 Belgian colts were born and raised at the farm.

Boulder Bridge showed its horses as extensively as its cattle. It exhibited National Champions—both stallions and mares—at the

Nelson Dayton, with his prize-winning Boulder Bridge Belgians, at the National Belgian Show, 1928

International Livestock Exhibition in Chicago and at the National Belgium Show at Waterloo, Iowa, in addition to the state fairs visited by the Guernseys. The farm's horses showed as well as its cattle did and won many prizes. In 1939, for example, the Society Royal Le Cheval de Trait Belge awarded the Belgian Breeders' Cup to Boulder Bridge Farm's Senior and Grand Champion mare, Astra de Cognebeau.

In 1937, when the department store no longer required horses for its delivery wagons, Nelson moved the delivery horses to the farm. Self-described farmhand Lloyd Mann drove one of the teams from Minneapolis along with all the gear from the city barn.

An employee at Boulder Bridge for 22 years, Mann later described the horses pulling a gangplow:

> It really was something to see those beautiful big horses in the field. That was one thing that Mr. Dayton liked to watch, and if I was plowing toward the road and he happened to be coming along in his automobile, he would stop and wait 'til I got to the road. He always had something nice to say about the horses. He didn't care how long it took to prepare the fields for planting as long as they looked nice. He generously said, "If you don't raise a crop this year, it won't be your fault."

Nelson sent Leslie Wilson to Belgium for his stallions and to the Isle of Guernsey for cattle, but his preference was to show, win, and sell livestock bred and raised at the farm, in contrast to his friend and state fair competitor Earle Brown, who simply bought and showed the best horses he could buy.

The farm had a well-rounded livestock program. In the next to the last year of its operation, for example, 503 purebred Doroc Jersey pigs were born and raised. This fine drift, or herd, was descended entirely from one sow. Shropshire sheep were part of the Boulder Bridge scene as well.

Superintendent Wilson felt that the combination of the farm's fine livestock and respect for its customers was the key to its repeat

Earle Brown

Sheriff Earle Brown, who inherited three fortunes and told Nelson that he "never spent half his income in a year," founded the highway patrol in 1929 and funded its first uniforms from his own pocket. Brown's Brooklyn (Center) Farms assembled a herd of Belgian horses that competed with Nelson's every year at the state fair. Nelson thought it was better to breed and raise great stock than to buy it, but because of their common interest in good horses, the two men became close friends. And Nelson's sons all came to know and respect "Mr. Brown."

Earle Brown

Earle Brown happened to come to the Dayton home for dinner just a day after the newspaper report of a local bank robbery. Nelson asked Brown to give the boys an eyewitness account of the event. Keeping the Dayton boys on the edge of their seats, Brown described the scene in some detail.

He and his deputy had driven into a little town and, noticing some commotion in front of the bank, stopped to ask what was going on. They learned that the bank had been robbed and the perpetrators had run off in a certain direction. The two lawmen quickly followed by car. Once the robbers were in sight, Brown took to the running board, firing at the robbers with his rifle. They stopped and Brown turned them in, then returned the money directly to the bank!

———

In 1932 the popular Sheriff Brown was drafted to run for governor, and Donald Dayton, then a student at Blake School, painted "Earle Brown for Governor" on the spare tires of his Buick. Alas, Brown lost the race in the national landslide electing Franklin Roosevelt!

Brown proved loyal when Bruce Dayton, later a director of Northwest National Life Insurance Company, requested some help. The Columbus, Ohio, group wanted to break off and invest in something its parent company thought was risky. Bruce, knowing Brown had a reasonable holding, asked him not to sell his shares. Brown answered, quickly, "I'll stick!'

Later, when Nelson's sons were trying to acquire land for the construction of the Brookdale indoor shopping mall in the Brooklyn Center area, Earle Brown again stood in their corner.

business. Indeed, customer loyalty was such that some time after one of the Nelson's bull calves killed the farmer who had bought him, his widow returned to Boulder Bridge with her new husband to get another one.

Nelson with Harold Ward at a farm outing for friends

Wilson was also proud that the farm trained many of the dairy industry's future leaders and of the "atmosphere of living" that Boulder Bridge provided to the 25 to 40 people working there.

Reporter Harry Woodworth gave a detailed picture of Boulder Bridge Farm in the September 1938 *Golfer and Sportsman,* noting among other things a neatly lettered black-and-white sign at its entrance: "Visitors Invited Every Day except Sunday." The farm's superintendent nevertheless gave dairy tours any day of the week. "You can't turn them down," he said, "because they have driven so far, even from other states."

Nelson welcomed all visitors wishing to tour the farm, and he frequently invited friends to dinner there. Once at a dinner party, someone said, "Mr. Dayton, if I had a farm like yours I'd never come to town."

"If you had a farm like mine," he replied, "you'd *have* to come to town."

Reporter Woodworth described the approach to Boulder Bridge as following: "After the entrance you pass the horse ring and stop in the center court, a clipped grass yard adjoining the horse barn, two cow barns, the bull [barn], the superintendent's office, the dairy, and three big stone silos." A poultry operation with a good-sized chicken house and housing for turkeys, geese, and ducks lay adjacent to the main farm.

The sire of the farm's original Guernsey herd was Warrior's Ace of Minnewashta. His successor in 1927 was Langwater Waldorf from Langwater Farm, Noreaston, Massachusetts, by this time one of the greatest sires of the breed. Langwater Waldorf beat every bull twice that beat him once in the ring.

Boulder Bridge farmhands had built two special boxcars, one for Guernseys, the other for the Belgians, to go on tour. The cattle were exhibited every year—except when the shows discontinued during World War II—at five or six state fairs and animal shows. In 1938, for example, the circuit included Illinois, Wisconsin, Iowa, and Minnesota state fairs, as well as shows at Waterloo, Iowa, and Columbus,

Langwater Waldorf beat every bull twice that beat him once in the ring.

Ohio, ending in December with Chicago's International Livestock Show. Guernseys had been sold into 13 different states.

No wonder! Boulder Bridge milk was of much higher quality than that required for certification. Its average bacteria count in 1939 ranged from 500 to 2,000 bacteria per cubic centimeter—9,000 under the maximum allowed for certification.

Superintendent Wilson said that lots of good, clean bedding was responsible for this showing. The main dairy barn contained 4 box stalls, 20 ties stalls, and 40 stanchions for the young cows and those not being regularly tested. Cows were groomed twice each day. Equipment, bottles, and milk cans were dry-heat sterilized. Employees in the milking barns wore professionally laundered white caps, shirts, and trousers.

Reporter Woodworth counted 78 cows on his 1938 visit to the farm, but Nelson's son Bruce remembers the number being closer to 200. The average worker hand-milked 10 to 12 cows at 4 A.M. and

4 P.M. Test cows were milked three times a day. At the one Boulder Bridge site using a milking machine, one man could milk 15 to 20 cows twice a day. One worker processed milk for delivery in cans or Guernsey bottles to the Dayton Company's Tea Room and restaurants—24 hours from cow to consumer. No milk was sold retail.

The farm bought about 2,000 chicks each year—White Leghorns and White Plymouth Rocks—to supply the Dayton residence and the farmhouse with poultry. About 600 pullets were kept for laying, and surplus winter eggs were marketed to Dayton's for its restaurants. There were also flocks of 350 turkeys, 25 geese, and 50 ducks.

Hampshire hogs were the most profitable department at Boulder Bridge. The farm had begun with four high-grade Hampshire sows and two Yorkshire sows—and a boar straight from the Ag School at the University of Minnesota. The hog farm was more than a mile from the farm's residences.

Boulder Bridge milk was of much higher quality than required for certification.

Boulder Bridge Farm preferred the use of unmechanized labor.

People and horses did the work of Boulder Bridge Farm where possible. The farm's original six mares and single stallion had become 56 purebred Belgians by 1938. Hitches of four to eight animals plowed and disked the ground, each pulling more than its own weight of about 2,000 pounds. Boulder Bridge blacksmith Angus McDonald shoed every one of the 56 Belgians every 60 days, taking about one hour per horse to do the job.

Mr. Wilson, who regularly wore a bow tie and a tweed cap, operated the farm much like any business—with a secretary, filing cabinets, telephones, and laboratories. The Boulder Bridge logo graced all the farm's advertising and at least some of its milk bottles.

In short, according to the *Golfer and Sportsman* writer Woodworth, Boulder Bridge was "a complete and rounded farm with the highest-grade methods, employees, animals, and marketing techniques." It raised as much produce as possible to avoid buying on the open market, and it performed as much of its work as it could—for example, butchering its own meat to feed the men at the farmhouse.

Boulder Bridge Farm

Woodworth closed by saying that Boulder Bridge Farm "served the two purposes [Nelson] had in mind . . . He established a country home for his family of five boys, and [he] is now maintaining herds of choice cattle and horses that enable farms to get seed stock developed for the benefit of [families in] Minnesota and its surrounding states."

By this time, Donald had graduated from Yale University and was working in the store. Bruce followed in his brother's footsteps at Yale, but even while he was away, Nelson kept him informed of some of the details of farm business.

In a February 5, 1937, letter to Bruce at the university, Nelson wrote: "Mr. Wilson is going down to New York tonight or tomorrow night for the American Guernsey Cattle Club Executive Committee meeting. We had a wonderful Guernsey cow offered to us the other day for $10,000. I would like to sell one for that price, but I can't

A classic "get" portrait, showing young Belgian horses born and raised at Boulder Bridge Farm.

imagine myself paying that much for one—$2,500 is the most we have paid yet for a cow, and I think it is enough."

Nelson continued to operate Boulder Bridge Farm, albeit a couple of years from his bed, until his death in 1950, 24 years after buying the original property. After he died, his sons sold the farm. Oldest son Donald explained: "We feared we might squabble more over the farm than we ever would over the store." Giving up the farm property was a mistake, says Bruce today—it could have become a beautiful park.

At any rate, Boulder Bridge Guernseys and other livestock were dispersed in October 1950 in the closing chapter of what has been described as "one of the greatest agricultural endeavors of modern times." Nelson had achieved there both his goals—mutually supportive—raising his boys in a wonderful place and improving the seed stock of farm families in the Midwest.

A *Minneapolis Star* editorial noted upon Nelson's death: "In agriculture he pursued an avocation—not as a gentleman farmer but as a practical college-trained scientist . . . His achievement in the breeding of cattle, horses, and swine made his Boulder Bridge Farm famous and helped to improve livestock throughout and beyond this region."

L. R. Lounsbury, editor of the *American Guernsey Breeders' Journal,* wrote:

> A great tribute was paid by the Guernsey Breeders of America to the late G. N. Dayton, owner, L. V. Wilson, manager, and Olaf Kjome, herdsman, when 1,600 gathered to witness the dispersal of the Boulder Bridge herd on October 6. The 158 animals of all ages sold [many to former customers] for $142,815, an average of more than $900, placing the sale among the outstanding dispersals of the Guernsey Breed. [The highest price for the day was $8,000 for Boulder Bridge Lucero ($71,264 in 2009 dollars).]
>
> When the last animal left the ring, the curtain fell upon a herd that was known from coast to coast and on an institution with a wonderful reputation for fair dealing, one that had contributed much to the Guernsey Breed.

The April 6, 1950, *Minnetonka Record* wrote of Nelson as a valued neighbor: "Boulder Bridge Farm has meant a great deal to all in Excelsior. During the dark days of the '30s, Boulder Bridge was kept 25 percent overstaffed on Mr. Dayton's orders . . . Much has been written of Mr. Dayton's accomplishments . . . But we write of him as our friend and neighbor."

As to the family aspects of Boulder Bridge, Nelson's son Ken, who once camped on nearby Wawatasso Island and sent smoke signals to his brothers at the farm, wrote many years later: "Boulder Bridge Farm was an absolutely glorious place at which to grow up. The combination of family, lake, and farm activities was a wonderful thing for five boys. We all thoroughly enjoyed it and loved it . . . It was a great life, a great place to raise a family. We had a ball."

Back row (l-r): Bruce, Nelson, and Donald; front row: Doug, Wally, and Ken (ca. 1930)

6

Family Man

While Nelson Dayton spent much of his time on business and farm, family simply came first.

A devoted son, Nelson demonstrated his love and respect for his parents in his arrangements for their economic welfare as well as in his thoughtful treatment of them day to day. He left the title "president" of The Dayton Company to his father the rest of George's life, even though Nelson owned 90 percent—or what he called "almost control"—and was wholly responsible for the business. He also paid his father a salary equal to his own—$75,000—especially important to George after he and Emma devoted much of their resources to development of the Dayton Foundation, then in the 1930s saw a major real estate development deal fail.

After attending morning services at Westminster Presbyterian church each Sunday they were in town, Nelson, Grace, and their sons often went to George and Emma's home for lunch. According to Ken, the Sunday lunch was always "a grand and glorious feast." Bruce re-

G. N. DAYTON FAMILY
Line of Descent

10)	Ralph Dayton	born 1588	in England
9)	Samuel	born 1635	Moved to East Hampton, Long Island
8)	Abraham	born 1665	
7)	Caleb	born 1686	
6)	Josiah	born 1714	
5)	Caleb	born 1735	
4)	Isaac Noble	born 1784	Moved to Western New York
3)	David Day	born 1811	Doctor, underground railway Druggist, tended blacks
2)	George Draper	born 1856	Moved to Worthington, MN 1883
Great	George Nelson	born 1886	
Grand	Donald C. Dayton Bruce B. Dayton Wallace C. Dayton Kenneth N. Dayton Douglas J. Dayton		born 1914-1924

Nelson descended from a long line of Daytons who paid great attention to family.

called "the best corn soup and spinach soufflé with mushroom sauce." After lunch the children played with one of two sets of blocks in the living room, so they could hear the discussions of the adults. When the boys were older, Nelson invited them to sit in on meetings of the Dayton Foundation, at which thank-you letters from its recipients were read.

George and Emma often visited Boulder Bridge Farm after attending services in town on summer Sundays. Bruce recalls walking on the long porch with his grandfather, who was always dressed in a suit. After Emma died in 1931, Nelson and Grace continued the Sunday lunches both at their home in Minneapolis and at Boulder Bridge Farm.

In 1926 Nelson's father was especially moved by some birthday surprises that Nelson and Grace planned for him from afar. George wrote them from Pasadena on March 7, the day after his 69th birthday: "Yesterday was a delightful day. Certainly I ought to be appreciative of all the kind acts and words. Thank you for the telegram, the flowers, the five books which all came on *the* day. If you could see that basket of flowers you would say (probably) as a number have said, "The most wonderful, or most beautiful, basket I ever saw."

One might think Grace took care of those arrangements, but Nelson did concern himself with such things, and he taught his sons about them as well. Later, in a letter to Bruce at Yale University, Nelson wrote: "Today is Aunt Caroline's birthday. Remember your mother's birthday comes on February 15th. Flowers are a very nice birthday remembrance but, in my opinion, not enough from you."

In February 1927, George wrote Nelson from his yearly vacation spot—the Huntington Hotel in Pasadena—asking which farms he would like to see while visiting there; they must have visited the farms together. Once, when Nelson was called out of town just before his purchase of an additional 40 acres for Boulder Bridge Farm, he asked his father, by then about age 75, to manage his closing on the Gifford piece. Upon Nelson's return, George handed him the papers and said, "I was glad to represent you on that purchase—it's a real piece of farmland."

Nelson was as attentive to his siblings. As a child, he looked up to and emulated his older brother, and as adults, the two operated harmoniously as the controlling owners and executives of The Dayton Company from 1911 to 1923. Whenever he looked back on his brother's death at age 43, Nelson was heartened to remember that Draper knew before he died that together they had reached their goal of surpassing Donaldson's and made Dayton's the preeminent department store of the region.

Nelson was devoted to his sisters, Caroline and Josephine. In 1922 Nelson and Draper arranged to obtain the one-twelfth interest of the business owned by each of their two sisters. Draper thought the price suggested by their father was too high, but Nelson persuaded him that George would never give them a chance to get that stock again. Thus they provided Caroline and Josephine with $150,000 of Dayton Company preferred stock for their $25,000 of common stock and agreed to pay them 8 percent on that stock for ten years, a generous arrangement. Draper insisted their agreement provide for an end to that payment should either brother die. After Draper died, Nelson continued the 8 percent payments to the end of the term, making that a condition for the sale of small amounts of common stock to store executives.

Nelson looked over his siblings' interests in other ways too. When Caroline decided to dissolve her marriage, for example, the family sent Nelson to Denver to handle her divorce. She returned to Minneapolis to live with and care for George after his beloved Emma died.

Draper and Nelson had agreed with each other that if either of them died, the survivor could obtain the other's common stock. Draper's papers indicated that $68 per share would be fair, but Nelson willingly paid Draper's family $80 per share, though that extended his debt for two decades.

George appreciated Nelson's advice and performance in augmenting the estates of all the members of his family. He wrote Josephine ca. 1936 regarding some recent financial arrangement: "I am glad Nelson suggested this to me and hope it will prove helpful to Caroline and Josephine, and someday something be left for the grandchildren who may then need it more than any of us need it now. Nelson has been very thoughtful in trying to plan for his father and each of his sisters in

Three of George's grandchildren: Doug, Wally, and Ken (ca. 1929)

Back row, l-r: Nelson and Grace with Bruce and Donald; front row: Doug, Ken, and Wally

various ways, so that we all may be a little more comfortable if financial losses should come." Certainly Nelson merited the trust his father showed in naming him sole executor of his estate.

As for his immediate family, Nelson was more than devoted, especially to his wife, Grace. They were partners with an easy, warm relationship—easy because they agreed on almost everything. One morning the two disagreed on some minor issue, had a little spat, and Nelson left for the store downtown. Ten minutes after he had driven down the road, he was back to work things out with Grace.

Nelson did not particularly enjoy being a public man, he didn't like to go out much, and he didn't like to go anywhere other than his business without Grace. In fact, he traveled little, but he did go annually to the Greenbrier Resort in White Sulphur Springs, West Virginia, for AMC meetings—and usually Grace went along. Nelson did not like flying, so they always took the train.

Grace was free to do whatever she wanted, but she knew better than to push. By far the more social of the two, she arranged everything to make Nelson's life happy—for example, answering the phone at home so that he wouldn't have to. Eager to do her part for the many organizations she supported, she nevertheless refused to be an officer of any for which she would have to be out in the evening. Nelson liked to be at home when he wasn't working, and Grace wanted to be home with Nelson whenever he was there. Occasionally Nelson attended musical events with Grace, but the only performances he enjoyed were the ice-skating shows at the Nicollet Hotel. He and Grace attended skating shows there many times together.

So family life centered in the home—whether in Minneapolis or at the Boulder Bridge family residence, both of which Grace managed and made comfortable. The Daytons employed a cook during much of their married life. Grace worked with the cook in planning meals to

Longtime housekeeper Christine Thune, preparing for a party

please her family and their guests. She tested a new cook the first night by asking for a thrifty dish that Nelson was fond of—sweet potatoes and bread cubes, made according to his mother's recipe.

Grace kept their homes, especially the one at Boulder Bridge, beautiful—with cut flowers from her abundant gardens there. Household helper Christine Thune was skillful in arranging the bounty.

Nelson and Grace presented a united front, especially in bringing up their children, born over a period of ten years: Donald Chadwick (August 13, 1914), Bruce Bliss (August 16, 1918), Wallace Corliss (March 12, 1921), Kenneth Nelson (July 20, 1922), and Douglas James (December 2, 1924). A daughter, Elizabeth died at birth on May 24, 1915.

As mentioned earlier, the Daytons made few requirements of the boys, as they believed that the only real influence a parent had was by example. They loved their sons, told them what was expected in a broad way, then gave them a lot of leeway about how to accomplish it. Grace objected to having the boys work in the store in the summer. She thought they might have enough of that later on. Nelson agreed—he was happy to have his sons active and working at the farm.

Nelson liked to have fun with the boys. Bruce remembered him playing tag with them in the early mornings, all in their pajamas, in the living room. He also recalled Nelson listening to the radio while he shaved and that Nelson liked a particular brand of toothpaste, named something like "Vividoo."

When Nelson asked for it at Dayton's department store, the clerk said, "We don't carry that anymore."

Nelson answered, "Oh, that was the best we ever had."

The clerk said, "Yes, but you and one other customer are the only ones who think so."

That reminded Nelson that he should leave buying to the buyers.

One of the few things Nelson drilled into the boys was to be careful about what they did so that they wouldn't end up on the front page

L-r: Doug, Ken, Wally, Bruce, and Don

of the newspaper: "The name of the store is the same as ours, so be careful. The Bells are not necessarily associated with General Mills, but in the eye of the public all of the Daytons are associated with Dayton's department store."

A man with both feet planted in the earth, Nelson disliked extravagance, and he often said that, especially in advertising, "only one thing can be superlative at one time." Exaggerated claims served only to destroy the meaning of words. And two other things Nelson taught again and again by example, both at the department store and at Boulder Bridge Farm: "Do only what you can do as well as it can be done anywhere," and "From those to whom much has been given, much is required—the only thing worse than a bum is a rich bum."

The Daytons taught their sons by example that hard work and a fair ethic brings success. Each son felt he had a great deal of freedom and, along with that, a great deal of trust. One thing they all knew—no matter what time they came in, they must go in and kiss their mother goodnight.

The Daytons believed the home and family influence was of more value to their children than any benefits that Eastern boarding schools might provide. They decided their sons would attend Blake School—"Little" or "Junior" Blake (grades 1–5) in Minneapolis and "Big Blake" (grades 6–12) in the Minneapolis suburb of Hopkins. The boys enjoyed their school days at Blake, worked hard, and all graduated well prepared for their college years.

The Daytons encouraged athletics, and all the boys took part in sports beyond their many physical pursuits at Boulder Bridge, though none particularly excelled in team sports. Oldest son Donald contracted polio at about age 13 while showing a calf at the Hennepin County Fair. (Grace thought all the boys had a little bit of it.) As a result, Don was the only one of the brothers who didn't serve in World War II. Still, he became captain of Blake's swimming team. Bruce was on the third line of the hockey team there.

Doug with Astra de Cognebeau, Senior and Grand Champion mare at the 1939 Minnesota State Fair

Nelson liked to walk wherever he was—in the city he walked the 16 blocks from home to work and back most days of the week. (He usually did not work Saturdays, and of course the store was closed on

Sunday.) He enjoyed walking alone, and sometimes he ducked around a corner to make sure he could continue without companions. Perhaps that commute on foot was his thinking time.

Donald wasn't able to walk as much after he had polio. So Nelson and Grace provided him with a buckboard wagon, basically a wood platform with four wheels, so that Donald could get around the Boulder Bridge neighborhood more easily.

Nelson was a golfer, though not a very good one—he went too far on his backswing—but he thought everyone should know how to play. Once he went too fast and too far with his backswing and that ended it for him. Doug recalled that once when he wanted to go north to the family cabin, Nelson asked him how he was doing with his golf quota: "I said, 'I'm 90 holes behind.' Father said, 'Make it up and you can go.'

"Well, I had a motor scooter, and Minnetonka Country Club was two miles down the road. It was 18 holes for a dollar, lunch, and another 18 holes for another dollar. I played 90 holes in one week. The only fun of it was trying to chase gophers with my putter!"

Donald, Bruce, and Ken were the golfers. Wally and Doug liked to ski and were enthusiastic hunters. Nelson did not hunt, though he shot squirrels, which he concluded could easily take a year's growth off a young tree. He also snared gophers when he thought they were making holes enough in the pastures to put his cattle in danger. Sometimes he asked the boys to help him get rid of the pests.

Vernon Benson drove the younger boys when they were in town, to Little Blake School, at 22nd and Colfax. He dropped the older boys at a corner of Franklin and Hennepin to take the streetcar to Big Blake. Bruce liked to stop on the way home at Lenz and Kelly's drugstore for a malt. That was at about 5:30, and the Daytons had dinner at 6:30. A malt was okay so long as he cleaned his plate at dinner.

During the school months when the family lived at Boulder Bridge Farm, Benson dropped off the boys directly at school. Bruce

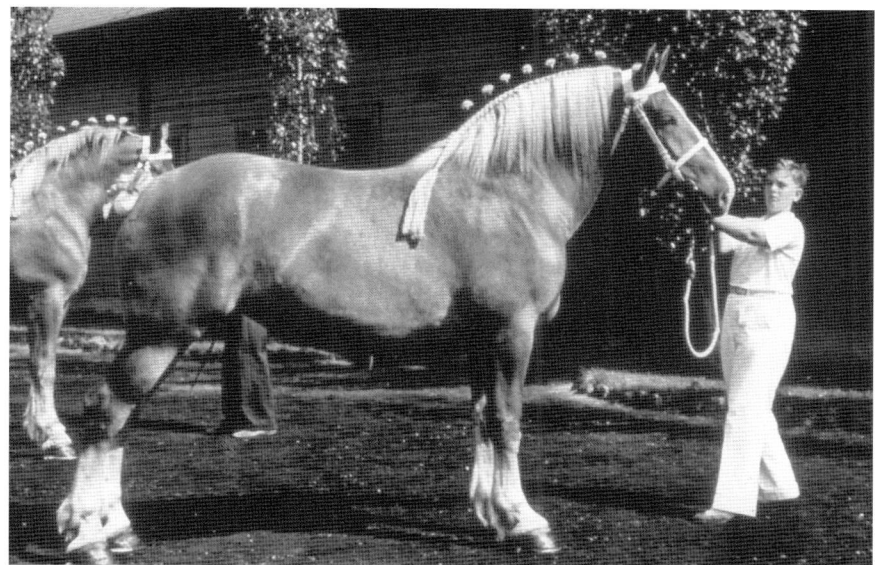

Ken with one of the prize Beligans

recalled that when he was 15 and first could drive, "I spent the first night of my birthday weekend with the family, and the next night I went into town for a movie. When I was dating Jane Pillsbury, Mrs. Pillsbury said, 'I know Bruce is a good driver because Vernon Benson trained him.'"

As to higher education, Nelson said he was willing to pay the cost of any college each of them might choose—*except* Harvard. His brother, Draper, had graduated from Princeton, and Nelson knew of some kind of a dispute between the two universities. Donald, Bruce, and Ken chose Yale University; Wally and Doug graduated from Amherst, one of the top liberal arts colleges in the country; and Nelson did pay their tuition. All the boys but Bruce, who majored in English, earned bachelor's degrees in history.

Nelson brought home a briefcase from work, and he often read the *Wall Street Journal* there. He was an avid reader, mostly of American history and biography. He didn't discuss his reading at the din-

Wally, Doug, and Ken

ner table, but he did speak often of his business both at the farm and at the store, and he did impart his knowledge of finance to at least one son.

Bruce recalls sitting in Nelson's lap when he was four years old, learning the difference between common and preferred stocks, between interest and dividends. One summer Bruce was reading the annual reports of General Mills and Pillsbury and mentioned that Pillsbury was one-third the size of General Mills. Nelson responded, "I would never want my competitor to be one-third my size."

Recognized as the financier of the five boys, Bruce received from his grandmother Emma Dayton a book of notes when he was quite young, and he began lending money to his brothers, sometimes at exorbitant rates of interest. On one occasion, Nelson judged the 25 cents his son charged on a $1 loan so exorbitant that he required Bruce to donate it to Westminster Presbyterian Church.

The Daytons threw few parties at home, and the boys attended none of them, though they often had guests for dinner. On one such occasion, Nelson demonstrated his dry wit in response to guest Dan Bull, president of Cream of Wheat. When Nelson finished saying grace before the meal, Bull said, "Nelson, I didn't hear a word you said."

Nelson replied, "Dan, I wasn't talking to you!"

Family birthdays were always family affairs. And for Fourth of July the Daytons might have some fireworks, a few rockets and sparklers at Boulder Bridge. Later the family enjoyed watching Fourth of July fireworks at the Lafayette Club.

In 1928, Nelson's parents celebrated their golden wedding anniversary, first with a party for employees at the store, then, according to George's *Autobiography:* "In the evening, at the home of Mr. and Mrs. G. Nelson [in Minneapolis], assisted by [Nelson's sisters] Caroline and Josephine, 700 invited guests called to congratulate and shake hands with Emma and George."

On another anniversary—Nelson and Grace's—Nelson told the boys they were going to have raw oysters, which they, or at least Wally, had never eaten before.

"Take one," Nelson said.

Wally declined, and Nelson again said, "Take one."

"No, thank you."

"Take just one."

Wally ate one. It went down, bounced, and came right back onto the table!

Nelson and Grace for many years never served liquor at home. But then Bruce came home from Yale wanting to throw a party at the Minneapolis Club. When his parents asked why he wanted the party there rather than at home, he said he wanted to serve cocktails. They talked it over, then told him he could serve cocktails at home. He had the party at home, serving liquor there with no ill effect. After that, Nelson occasionally drank an Old Fashioned, Grace a glass of sherry, before dinner at home.

Granelda

In 1932, the height of the Great Depression, a Sunday school classmate of Nelson's from Worthington—Burr Ludlow—let Nelson know he dealt in northern Minnesota real estate. Nelson said he might be interested in buying there should Ludlow find something appropriate for him. The enterprising Ludlow found a cabin foreclosed by an Indiana bank with a mortgage of $6,500. On Memorial Day weekend, 1932 or '33, Nelson put all five of his sons in the car and drove to Lake Vermilion, about five miles from Cook, Minnesota, to see the place.

Nelson was impressed with the beautiful, pine-forested property fronting on the 36-mile-long lake—as were all the members of the family when they saw it—and he bought it for the cost of the mortgage. He used another $6,500 to bring the plumbing and electricity up to date. After the improvements were made, Nelson and Grace drove north from the Twin Cities to try it out. Grace loved it, but when nothing seemed to work, Nelson went home disappointed. He didn't return for three years. Grace said, "Little things like that bothered Nelson, but he was awfully good on the big ones."

Eventually, Nelson went back to the cabin with Grace. They had a good time and afterwards made repeated visits together. They dubbed the property Granelda (a shortened combination of *Gra*ce and *Nel*son *Da*yton). Every boat owned by Nelson's family, including those at Boulder Bridge Farm and Granelda, has since borne the name *Grace B.*

Nelson and Grace never visited Granelda with the whole family. But later the five sons made regular, separate visits to Granelda with friends and family members. Wally loved the cabin and its environs so much that he took over its management. He and his wife, Mary Lee Lowe Dayton, later developed an excellent book on wildflowers in the area. The cabin has never been altered or expanded. The property, with about four miles of shoreline, will someday go to the Minnesota Department of Natural Resources.

Grace's favorite photo of herself, by the boathouse at Granelda

The Long Pull

The Dayton family lived at a succession of addresses in Minneapolis. With his father at 2020 Blaisdell, Nelson and Grace lived at 2100. After Draper died, Nelson moved to Draper's house at 2321 Blasdell, three blocks from the Minneapolis Institute of Arts, which proved much to Bruce's delight. Nelson tore down the house at 2100 and, to open up the space, gave the land to his father. After the boys became adults, Nelson realized he wouldn't be there much longer, and he wanted Grace to be settled in a nicer place in town. They sold the residence at 2321, then bought and moved to a more comfortable home on Franklin Avenue and Knox.

Whenever any of the Daytons was away—or when he was away himself—Nelson wrote often. When his sons were away at Yale and Amherst and when they were serving in the military during World War II, he wrote them about once a week, sometimes to more than one son at a time. Usually the letters were typed, so he probably dictated them to a secretary at his office. He wrote on a wide range of topics, many of which have been discussed earlier.

As to family business, Nelson wrote Bruce at Yale in February 1937:

> Enclosed herewith you will find a check of The Okabena Company for $100.00. Last fall I transferred to each of the five boys one share of stock in The Okabena Company. We paid a dividend of $100.00 a share this month. We were going to elect Donald a director of The Okabena Company, and it [was] necessary for him to have one share of stock to qualify as a director. He is now a director of the Boulder Bridge Farm Company and in The Okabena Company, and we elected him second vice president of The Okabena Company without any salary.

Knowing that many people had trouble bringing together the controlling interest in a family company, Nelson had started The Okabena Company in the 1920s to bring the majority of the common stock of The Dayton Company together; eventually he controlled 90 percent of it. He knew Boulder Bridge Farm Company would never make a lot of money but that it was a good asset to pass on to his sons. He awarded each of the five a 9 percent interest in the farm amounting to 45 percent, but he kept the remaining 55 percent and full control during his lifetime.

Today Okabena Company tends to the joint business interests of Dayton family members.

Nelson signed the letter to Bruce at Yale and other letters to his sons "Daddy," and his sons addressed him that way in person and whenever they spoke of him, at least when they were younger. Nelson preferred that title as warmer and more respectful than the shorter "Dad" and in contrast to his own father's wish to be addressed as "Father."

Nelson was as kind and generous to his in-laws as to his parents. Grace's brother, Frank Bliss, died in an auto accident in 1917, leaving his widow and four children with little financial means. Nelson and Grace, in only their fifth year of marriage, took on the financial support of Frank's family through college (one through medical school) for the children and the lifetime of his widow. When the youngest child reached school age, his mother took on a part-time job, but the Daytons persuaded her that the children would be better off with her at home. The younger Blisses often noted the influence their Uncle Nelson and Aunt Grace had on their development.

Grace's father, Cortis Bliss, was a tall, handsome man who occasionally visited the Daytons, making great fun for the boys. He slept in the guest room, always with his toes sticking out, and the boys liked to sneak in and tickle his feet. The whole family enjoyed maple syrup from Cortis's farm in Vermont on their pancakes. When Cortis died, Nelson took the whole family to Mitchell, South Dakota, for his funeral. He told his sons that his father-in-law was a good man.

Nelson never did take his family to visit his hometown of Worthington, though he clearly recalled his own days there with fondness. On April 8, 1942, he wrote to Ken:

The train tomorrow will take us through Worthington. It will be the first time I have been down there for 20 years or more. The town has grown a lot since we left. There were about 2,800 people there then and now there are close to 6,000. They have some big hatcheries there and call themselves the "Turkey Capitol of the World."

I imagine there are only two or three families there whom I know. I wish I had a chance to walk up around our old house. When we lived there, there was only one other house in our block. Later Father sold another corner out of the block, but now several houses are in that block . . .

I'd like to have about an hour down there tomorrow. Instead of the five minutes which the train stops.

Nelson seems to have had a special feeling for his daughters-in-law, too. Not all of the boys married before Nelson's death, but Ken's wife, Judy (Julia Winton Dayton), recalls having met Nelson before she and Ken ever dated. As editor of the Northrop Collegiate School yearbook—*The Tattler*—she approached Nelson in his office on the ninth floor of Dayton's, hoping he would buy a full-page ad as he had in past years. When she asked, he "looked me in the eye and said, 'Why should I do that?'"

Unable to think of any other answer, she answered, "Because you always have." That was good enough, and he bought it.

Wally's wife, Mary Lee, recalled Nelson's response to their engagement: "My parents were in Michigan for the summer. Wally called his father, and we went over to his parents' home. Father had gone to bed. He arose, got all dressed up—down to the cufflinks—to come down and congratulate us."

Then, she said, "For our first Christmas with our daughter Sally, we went to my parents' home for Christmas and then my family all went to Christmas dinner with the Daytons—and then for the Sunday lunches, too."

According to Judy, Grace continued the Christmas get-togethers and welcomed the little ones even when they had a fever. Once when grandson Judd had an upset tummy, Grace let him eat his molded ice-cream Santa with a little salt spoon. Christine Thune said, "Don't swallow that. We only have 11."

All of the Dayton sons and their families eventually lived at Lake Minnetonka—except for Bruce, who lived near Long Lake. After Nelson died, Donald, Bruce, Wally, Ken, and Doug carried on with Grace certain of the family traditions that Nelson loved as well as made new ones of their own.

Longtime Dayton Company employee E. S. Larsen summed up Nelson's devotion to his family in describing how Nelson kept George's office, even after his death: "It was carefully dusted early every morning . . . [Nelson] never discussed why his father's office was maintained so long . . . but unquestionably it was a matter of sentiment, for this man loved his father and mother and his own family more than anything on this earth."

Westminster Presbyterian Church, Minneapolis

7

Presbyterian, Citizen, Philanthropist

Nelson Dayton was a faithful Presbyterian, an active citizen of Minneapolis and Minnesota, and a generous, thoughtful giver. His participation on each of these fronts informed and enriched each of the others, and he and Grace taught their sons by example their religious, civic, and philanthropic practice. In these things, too, they lived out the principle of doing what they could "as well it can be done anywhere." Their daughter-in-law Mary Lee Lowe Dayton, also the daughter of their Presbyterian minister, noted that the whole family was grateful for its blessings and eager to give back to its larger community.

Reared in both his father's Presbyterian and his mother's Methodist faiths, plus whatever Christian revival meeting might visit Worthington, Nelson had heard many times the story of how he was named for the missionary in Syria whose family his parents supported for many years. From the tithing-at-least practice of his parents, he learned that he was expected to do his part. Nelson and his brother and sisters donated part of their allowances and earnings to the Westminster

Presbyterian Church of Worthington and to the larger church's mission efforts.

Nelson was as down to earth about religion as about everything else in his life. He later told his sons, "My father was a religious fanatic. I never believed half that stuff." Perhaps not, but Nelson's daughters-in-law Judy and Mary Lee, when asked to describe him, both started with the word *religious*. Whether or not Nelson picked up the creed, he certainly took on the values informing Emma and George's spiritual lives. And he demonstrated those values in the way he treated others, in the ethics he lived out in his business and civic life, and in the gratitude with which he shared his bounty.

Shortly after their wedding, it may be remembered, Nelson and Grace visited several Minneapolis churches of their respective persuasions, finally settling on Westminster Presbyterian Church of Minneapolis at the corner of Nicollet Mall and 12th Street South. Nelson's parents, Emma and George, transferred their memberships to Westminster in 1925.

Nelson played an active role in his church of choice. In March 1915, just a few months after his first son, Donald, was born, George wrote Nelson while on a trip to Washington, D.C.: "I cannot tell you the pleasure it gives your father and mother to learn [through] the *Tribune* this morning that you were elected a deacon last Thursday evening . . . The church falls far short of its privilege and duty, but still it accomplishes much."

Nelson's boys early became aware of their parents' daily spiritual practice—morning prayer for the whole family, usually the reading of a psalm or other Bible verse. And Nelson always said grace before dinner. As the Dayton boys became old enough, their parents introduced them to Westminster's Sunday school, where Grace was a beloved teacher. Later they attended services with their parents.

Youngest son Doug once recalled "sitting there during the Sunday service, looking straight ahead with my mind a hundred miles away."

Nelson admitted the quality of preaching was not consistent, in a letter to Bruce at Yale (February 5, 1937):

> Mr. Berlis preached last Sunday. We all stayed home. Mother had promised the boys they could have one Sunday off while we were east. When we did not go, they still wanted their Sunday off. She persuaded them to go as long as Dr. Boddy preached and then let them off last Sunday. Berlis will preach again next Sunday morning, and I presume we will all hear him. They say he did a good job last Sunday.

The whole family took Sundays off from church during the Boulder Bridge "season," but when they were in the city, both Nelson and Grace were active at Westminster. Nelson was a trustee (1924–1950) and the chair of the trustees for a period (1941–1946), and he gave the church generous financial support. As a result of his involvement there, he became active at Abbott Hospital, which was owned by the church; he served on the hospital board and for a time was its chair.

When Nelson's father gave the Westminster Presbyterian Church the funding for a chapel, Grace served on the building committee with Franklin Crosby (of Washburn-Crosby Company—later General Mills), also a trustee. After one meeting, Crosby told Nelson, "Grace has great ideas, Nelson, but they're all expensive." Nelson cracked later in another setting that Franklin's brother, John Crosby, looked "like a petrified mummy, but he was sharp as a tack."

By the time the renovations at Westminster were done, George was in his last year and could no longer walk or climb stairs on his own. He wrote Nelson's sister Caroline in September 1937 after the new chapel and parish house were complete: "I have just come from a trip through the new church. Grace and Nelson were there to pilot me—John had brought up the wheelchair from the store so that I could be wheeled around [I was carried up and down the stairs] . . .

Franklin M. Crosby

Grace made a wonderful leader because she knew all the rooms and the various purposes for which they are needed."

Nelson did his share for the national denomination as well. He served as board member and for a time president of the Presbyterian Foundation for Home Missions, and he was a member of the Board of National Missions from 1938 to 1942. He believed that even such a good cause should not benefit from people's bad habits and was surprised to learn that the foundation owned stocks in liquor and tobacco companies. He nevertheless continued to enjoy an occasional Old-Fashioned before dinner—and an E & E cigar afterwards.

Nelson was a good citizen who kept an eye out for his larger community for both humanitarian and business reasons. He knew that a healthy city, state, and nation could best support the store. Very early and through his career with Dayton's, he became involved in organizations including the Minneapolis Retailers Association, Minneapolis

Chamber of Commerce, the Better Business Bureau, and the Minneapolis Advertising Club. Always a booster for Minneapolis, he frequently spoke at their meetings. He was also a member of the downtown Minneapolis Club.

An unidentified 1917 news clipping indicates that Nelson was called as a member of the Minneapolis Retailers Association to "the Washington meeting of the economy board of the council of national defense" to advise with others on the most efficient means for "wartime mobilization of all resources." He obliged, of course. After training at Fort Snelling, he served in the U.S. Army Reserves.

Both Nelson and his father served as directors of Northwestern National Bank before and during the Great Depression, when banks could have as many directors as they wished. After Franklin D. Roosevelt enforced restrictions as to the number of directors (so that they would take greater responsibility for bank operations), Northwestern trimmed its board, retaining both Nelson and George.

As directors of Northwestern National Bank, father and son participated in plans for Northwest Bancorporation (later Norwest, today part of Wells Fargo), a holding company designed to make duly profitable the banks it held in the region. George served as a director from the start of the group's active life, on February 19, 1929, until June 1935, when he resigned due to illness. Nelson was elected in his place.

Before the Great Depression, Nelson said it was not an honor to be a bank director but a disgrace *not* to be one. Three of his sons—Don, Ken, and Bruce—served as bank directors at some time in their careers. Nelson claimed that bank board meetings were the best place to learn the town gossip, far beyond any women's bridge party.

Having come to the city from Worthington, Nelson was always respectful of the top families in Minneapolis. One fellow director at Northwestern after some time grew tired of Nelson's usual greeting: "Good morning, Mr. Pillsbury."

"Nelson, when are you going to call me John?" Pillsbury responded.

John S. Pillsbury Jr.

After that rebuke, Nelson always addressed him as "John."

Well-respected himself, Nelson was also a director of Northwestern National Life Insurance Company (no connection to the bank), serving 11 years. He was also a trustee at Blake School from 1927 to 1942. He became a member of the regional Agricultural Credit Corporation in 1932. And for more than 30 years he played an active part in the YMCA, serving at various times on its advisory board and on its building, central branch management, world service, and Camp Ihduhapi committees.

Nelson was a member of the board of directors of the Boy Scouts (1929–1934) and of the board of the Council of Social Agencies (1935–1940). From 1942 to 1946, the Community Fund became part of Hennepin County's War Chest, which supported war-related relief and service activities; for three years (1943–1946) he served on the War Chest's board of directors, as well as on its national and international agencies' committees.

The radio Nelson listened to while shaving every morning was always tuned to the news. He enjoyed a good political contest, and he was a prominent contributor to the state GOP. In tune with the two-year election cycles of the time, he met with Sydney Anderson, vice president and political point man for General Mills, in the General Mills room at the Minneapolis Club to decide on which Republican they would back for governor. After some discussion, they agreed on a candidate, and each pledged a generous amount of support.

Nelson said, "The man you support in politics will always disappoint you, but hopefully he will do better than his opponent."

Nelson knew Stassen from the time Harold was a student, working part time at the Dayton's first branch store at the University of Minnesota. A Dayton's advertisement in the *Minnesota Daily* informed undergraduates that if they wanted to see man-about-campus "Red" Stassen on that particular day, he would not be in the offices of the *Law Review* or in

Cmdr. Harold E. Stassen, USNR

any of the places he frequented as a student, but at Dayton's University Store helping fellow students choose slacks, sports jackets, and such.

Nelson was the first major supporter of Stassen, who won the governorship in 1938, 1940, and 1942 and served from 1939 to 1943, when he resigned for World War II service. Nelson also supported Stassen's first foray into national politics.

Stassen wrote to Nelson on at least two occasions in the late 1940s. In October 1947 he reported completion of the "first two-year period of our national campaign . . . There is every indication in recent polls and comments of Republican leaders that we are in an excellent position . . . My recent [campaign] journey through New England sparkled with good news. This favorable standing today is due in large measure to the early backing of yourself and others." He ended the letter by thanking Nelson "for your significant assistance during this critical period."

After the 1948 GOP convention, at which Dewey won the presidential nomination that Stassen had sought, Stassen wrote thanking Nelson for his "exceptional assistance during the campaign" and saying that he would continue his work to strengthen "the more liberal and humanitarian views [of] the Republican Party."

Nelson also paid attention to the cultural aspects of his community, realizing they were important to the community whether he was personally interested in them or not. Though he was not a sports fan in general (there were no professional league teams in Minneapolis then), he was loyal to his alma mater's football team, and he did have season tickets to the Minnesota Gopher games, particularly when Bernie Bierman was their coach (1932–1941 and 1945–1950). Nelson was also a member of the Minikahda, Woodhill, and Lafayette Clubs, all of which promoted golf.

As to other cultural activities, Nelson said, "There are two things I don't give a hoot about, but I know they're good for the community"—art and music. So he gave generously to the Minneapolis

Symphony Orchestra and the Minneapolis Institute of Arts because he believed they distinguished Minneapolis from the "typical" midwestern town.

Grace enjoyed going to the orchestra's performances regularly, and she took Nelson along whenever he agreed to go. Once asked to serve on the symphony association's board, Nelson declined but said his son Kenneth liked Brahms and might do so. Ken said later that he liked just about all kinds of music—he and his brothers learned about classical music through a great stack of records played on the family phonograph. Ken accepted the board seat, going on to serve what is now the Minnesota Symphony for many years.

As for the Minneapolis Institute of Arts, Nelson's son Bruce regularly walked the three blocks from 2321 Blaisdell to the museum on Third Avenue South, quite interested on his own. He never visited the museum with Nelson, but occasionally his mother accompanied him. At one museum event, the institute's president—Alfred Pillsbury—was greeting guests, and when Grace and Bruce approached him, he said, "Young man, I have something in mind for you." Bruce didn't learn what Mr. Pillsbury had in mind until he was in the army. When he returned home from service in World War II, he was invited to his first meeting as a trustee of the institute. He accepted the invitation. "No doubt," he says, "my father's generosity to the museum was a factor in my appointment." Bruce is still an institute trustee.

Nelson knew all the top people in the Twin Cities and so was an important resource for fundraising. In 1933 Weaver Dobson, the brother-in-law of Grace's best friend from Mitchell, was named head of the Community Fund (United Way), one of Nelson's regular causes. Dobson asked his brother John to ask Nelson to head the "A list" of leading givers, that is, to solicit gifts from others.

Nelson, knowing Dobson's mission, played along, inviting him to dinner at the farm. During that evening, Nelson kidded Dobson, giving him the runaround. But when asked to take the lead fundrais-

James Ford Bell

ing position—tough enough any time, but especially so in the middle of the Great Depression—Nelson accepted. Soon he made his first call—on James Ford Bell, the head of General Mills. They agreed to give $10,000 each, a huge amount at the time, setting the standard for that year's giving.

In anticipation of great local need, the Dayton Foundation (see page 154) had voted a grant of $12,000 to the Community Fund. Unable to give personally what he had in the past, George was proud that Nelson was part of the campaign leadership, despite its taking him from the store.

George wrote daughter Josephine and her husband, Frederic Blair, who then lived in California, on October 14, 1933:

> Nelson is chairman of the "A" list. Of course, he did not want it but took it simply because our board of directors felt he owed it to the community to do so. It means an enormous amount of work for him up to November 10th. When he consented to act, he was told the rating had been completed, but he found out that was a mistake,

and for some days he and others have been wrangling with the question of how to rate individuals.

The amount to be raised is $1,650,000—the "A" group is supposed to raise about 55 percent of this. The "A" group is composed of those who give $500 or over and consists of about 500 individuals. It means that the "A" group must raise nearly $1 million. The balance is to be raised from about 93,000 persons, assuming that as many give as did last year.

Of course, it is a difficult problem this year to guess how different individuals are affected by the economic situation. Dobson is general chairman of the campaign, and he is going at it in a splendid way. He is about Nelson's age, and they make a splendid team and pull together well.

I regret exceedingly that Nelson is burdened with this, but someone had to take it, and the feeling seemed to be that it was his turn this year—perhaps the worst year of all the years in which the Community Fund has been raised.

Thereafter George reported Nelson's progress on a regular basis. Two weeks later, he wrote again to Josephine:

I wish you and Frederic could have heard Nelson last Tuesday evening at the "A" list dinner of the Community Fund—and also this noon as he presided at the luncheon for the "A" list solicitors . . . He was dignified, logical, without any ballyhoo, and handled himself in a way that made a deep impression . . .

It is tremendous to think of the same amount being raised as last year under all the circumstances. I believe this campaign will be a blessing to both Nelson and to Weaver, although it is pulling on their vitality and testing them physically to the utmost.

Store executive E. S. Larsen wrote later that Nelson presented the Community Fund drive at the store "stressing the debt owed to the community that gave it patronage . . . This was a matter of reciprocity . . . The store always gave substantial sums, and its management urged department managers and executives to give generously. Putting over the subscription to the Community Fund was done as carefully and with as much energy as was applied to any big sale for the store."

Nelson and Grace also participated in George and Emma's largest philanthropic endeavor. Nelson and his siblings had learned of their parents' intent to start their Dayton Foundation long before they incorporated it in 1918. This was their personal endeavor, not related to The Dayton Company. Seven years earlier the two had transferred the land beneath part of the store (at the Seventh Street Corner) to an account meant to fund the foundation. Dayton's Department Store paid $50,000 year rent on the land fast becoming the heart of downtown. For many years it was a major source of income to the foundation.

George and Emma invited each of their children to be part of the board of the foundation. One of its first acts after incorporation was to award an annual salary of $1,000 to the Rev. William S. Nelson of Tripoli, Syria, in support of his work for the Foreign Board of the Presbyterian Church. This was the man for whom Nelson Dayton was named. After Emma's death, Grace joined the board, and after George's death, Nelson became its president. Through the years, they opened the many letters from people requesting or thanking them for funds and decided how to respond to each. The Dayton boys heard the letters and the conversations about them at family/foundation meetings following the Daytons' Sunday lunches. Giving was simply a part of their lives.

Nelson and Grace, in an example of their constant outlook for the good of the community, took the opportunity when moving from their home on Blaisdell to the residence on Franklin to donate at few furnishings to the Minnesota Governor's Residence in St. Paul. Among the items they provided is a breakfront still in use at the residence on Summit Avenue that their grandson—Gov. Mark Dayton—occupies today.

In 1946, The Dayton Company became the second company in the United States to give 5 percent of its pretax profits—the most the government allowed it to deduct tax free—to charitable (in this case, local) causes including the Minneapolis Symphony, the Minneapolis Institute of Arts, the United Way, and many others. That practice continues into the 21st century through both Target Corporation and Target Foundation giving.

Laysha Ward, of Target Corporation, grateful for the good that Target and the Target Foundation continue to fund, wished recently to thank the Dayton family in person. She called on Bruce Dayton to express her appreciation for Nelson's initiation and the Dayton brothers' continued high standard for corporate giving to their community.

Shortly before Nelson died, he and Grace started their own foundation—Granelda—using the same combination of names titling their cabin at Lake Vermilion. Like George and Emma, they named their children among its trustees, and Nelson left 10 percent of his estate to the foundation, his sons to decide how to use those assets. Eventually the Granelda Foundation and the Dayton Foundation were combined into the Dayton Hudson Foundation; finally they became part of the Target Foundation of today.

Early in Nelson's store career, when the store was quickly expanding, George had worried about the effect of wealth on his descendants. When The Dayton Company capitalized its surplus by issuing preferred and common stock, he congratulated, then warned Draper and Nelson in a letter sent from Grove Park Inn in Asheville, North Carolina:

> I congratulate you both on all it means to you.
>
> And yet—be patient with me—I find myself hoping and praying it may not prove a curse to you or any of your children. To be sure you will have as a result of this decision not more wealth (aside from saving possible taxes on dividends heretofore declared), but it seems more definite, more tangible, more real. And when I think of the large wealth that is now yours as assured by this decision, it al-

most overwhelms me with the desire that there may come upon you, your wives, and your children such a keen sense of responsibility of stewardship, and of privilege as will drive you to your knees to seek the divine assistance and guidance as you consecrate yourselves and your all to his service. What tremendous opportunities are yours if thus consecrated . . .

I have realised for many years that large wealth was not best for me, and I can truly say God has graciously spared me some of the temptations that will come to you and your families—don't misunderstand me, I have had all the temptations I could resist and would not have resisted many without His help.

As I see the effect of wealth upon most families, I say "God forbid that my children, or any of my grandchildren, shall be cursed because of the abundance of material prosperity."

Occasionally, there is a family that is sobered by a sense of the great obligation indicated in "From those to whom much is given, much shall be expected, required." God help you and yours.

George needn't have worried. Nelson and Grace truly believed the adage "From those to whom much is given, much is required." They were grateful for their blessings and shared them freely. They made little show of their dedicated leadership in the city's religious, civic, and philanthropic life, but over time Minneapolis took note. In January 1950 the Community Chest and Council presented its Distinguished Community Service Award to the two Daytons, the first time it was awarded to a couple.

According to the *Minneapolis Star*, on April 1, 1950, the day of Nelson's death, "A quiet, retiring man whose modesty veiled much of his philanthropy and civic enterprise, Mr. Dayton did much to stimulate liberal public giving in Minneapolis . . . So great was the confidence of the Minneapolis business community in Nelson that most businessmen went along with [any] projects that bore his endorsement."

Nelson Dayton

8

The Long Pull

Nelson Dayton had many interests beyond The Dayton Company, but those rarely superseded his leadership of Dayton's Department Store. Looking to the future but maintaining his 90 percent interest, Nelson brought his oldest son, Donald, into the business in August 1937, a few months before George's death.

Nelson had never said to his sons, "I want you to come into the store," but the business had served him well, and he assumed it would serve them too. Donald evidently thought likewise.

Fresh out of Yale with a degree in history, Donald started as a stock boy at Dayton's just in time to watch his father manage the first expansion of the store in the wake of the Great Depression. Later described by reporters as the most intense of the brothers, Donald was quick to grasp problems even in areas with which he was unfamiliar, and he proved an ability to get people pulling together.

Donald worked his way quickly to the executive office next to his father's, and they met every day. Over the next decade Donald became

Donald Dayton

the glue holding Dayton's Department Store together. His management style blended seat-of-the pants daily decisions with a sense for excellence and merchandising wisdom.

Donald had a lot to learn, but he also had a superior role model and teacher. Nelson had kept Dayton's healthy enough through the depression that afterwards it could seize the opportunity to grow. And Donald immediately saw his father patiently negotiate for the Eighth and Nicollet property under J. B. Hudson, make the most of the publicity, and close the deal.

Over the next three years, Nelson conducted, with enthusiastic assistance from Donald, the construction on that corner of 4 additional floors—for a total of 7 floors—in another step towards George's 12-story vision. They also added 6 floors—for 10 floors total—to the parking ramp. The added space allowed expansion of several departments plus improvement of the tearooms and other services. Air-conditioning of the old quarters and most of the new gave, according to a timely ad, "our patrons in Minneapolis and the Northwest as complete facilities for their shopping as are enjoyed in any city in this country."

With its expanded physical area, the store offered more than ever in the way of merchandise and service. Just one example: From Dayton's earliest years, American actresses on tour often waited to reach the Twin Cities to buy a new fur coat. In 1939 Nelson engaged Dorothy Gavin to expand the sales of another kind of outdoor clothing—more and better sports clothes. Gavin explored every possibility—bathing suits, riding habits, fishing costumes, everything—and bought those with stylistic flair. She did this so well that Dayton's often retained the customers who bought its sportswear even after they moved from the community. And Gavin was the one woman of the time to become a divisional merchandise manager.

In the first stages of this revolution, young people were Dayton's most active customers. Now, in ever-growing numbers, they came to the new Town and Country section of the store. When Hugh Arthur came up with the phrase "Sun Fun," another division sprang into being. In the winter, it became "Snow Fun." Then, following the doctrine of C. J. Larson that "your business is as big as the glasses you look through," Dayton's created the Budget Shop for sportswear buyers. As the result of such innovation, Dayton's sales climbed from $17 million in 1938 to almost $20 million in 1941.

In 1940, Nelson's son Bruce graduated from Yale with a degree in English and a deep interest in matters of finance, and he joined

A Dayton's Sun Fun display

the company in 1940—though not for long. The world was in turmoil, and after Japan attacked Pearl Harbor on December 7, 1941, the United States was at war again. Grappling with shortages and a diminished staff due to 314 employees (including Bruce) being off to war, Nelson continued the drive to deepen Dayton's market dominance.

Over the next four years, three other of Nelson's sons—Wallace, Kenneth, and Douglas—also joined the armed services. Bruce served what he called "an undistinguished career" in the United States, France, and Germany, with the Germans surrendering two days after he arrived in France. Wally, who earned a degree in history at Amherst, served as a naval officer on a supply ship in the Pacific. Ken was a sergeant in Gen. George Patton's tank corps, which went as far as Czechoslovakia before being forced to pull back to Germany.

Doug saw the most action, in 1943 spending eight months in Ireland before landing in France on D-Day + 30, participating in the Battle of the Bulge, and contracting yellow jaundice. Wounded in battle, he was sent to England, out of harm's way. Because of that, he called the injury his "million-dollar-wound."

In the meantime, Donald, classified 4-F because of his earlier struggle with polio, assisted in moving the company forward. Though at first things seemed to be normal, American industry was being drawn into the worldwide conflict. Goods were scarce because many basic materials also went to war. Familiar commodities ceased to exist—appliances, for example, because they were transformed directly into weapons, and silk stockings, because the stuff of which they were made was needed for ropes, tires, and powder bags. As the war went on, the competition for goods heightened. Some manufacturers became imperious, putting even their oldest customers on allotments and dictating all the terms of sale.

So, for years having worked primarily as a seller, the retailer suddenly became primarily a buyer. One Daytonian, whose realm was silk, hired a private plane and covered suppliers in three towns in North Carolina in a day and thought he had procured goods in all three. He was home only ten days when he learned that most of his orders were canceled. Someone of less scrupulous method had seized the merchandise.

Of course, not every source was whimsical. And Dayton's credit in the world of buying and selling was higher than ever. A generous share of ready-for-the-counter goods flowed into its receiving room, and where finished goods were scarce, resourceful Daytonians contrived them. They bought lumber, textiles, whatever the basic commodity, and arranged for the production of items to their specification by new manufacturers.

Trade came easily because the work was not in persuading people to buy but in providing the goods they clamored for. The expanded store's volume shot up, even though in 1943 it had to call off its annual Daisy Sale and its *Jubilee!*—because the government asked retailers not to promote the sale of textiles and textile products.

Nevertheless, the bankers of Minneapolis soon had evidence of how well Dayton's turned wartime crises to assets. To help finance its expansion program, The Dayton Company had borrowed $1,200,000 from the First National Bank and Trust Company of Minneapolis, its note secured by a mortgage on the company's real estate holdings. The terms of the loan called for repayment of $37,500 on each March 1 and September 1, beginning in 1940, until September 1, 1949, when the remainder—$487,500—was due. Nelson quietly paid three installments at a time, continuing so that on March 1, 1944, the debt was gone.

Upon notice of another triple payment in 1942, Lyman Wakefield of First National Bank wrote Nelson: "We congratulate you on being able to make the payment but regret that we have to take the money."

Another aspect of wartime business was that of the government establishing itself as a silent partner in all transactions. The Office of Price Administration (OPA), created to battle inflation through the control of commodity prices, cast a shadow unfamiliar to operators used to acting on their own. On receipt of the first OPA orders, Nelson called a meeting of all who could be affected by the agency's rulings: "Gentlemen, I shall expect you to abide not merely by the letter but by the spirit of the law." Donald often acted as Nelson's deputy in these matters, but eventually there emerged a staff of liaisons to work with the government in the fight against inflation.

To ensure that prices not threaten the war economy, the government also asked that retailers take a "base period" before the war as a standard and use only the historic markup. The purpose was simple, but interpretation of the original law and subsequent directives was so complicated as to require translation. One employee virtually lived with the OPA directors in St. Paul, using the rest of his time to translate their words for the laypersons at Dayton's.

Still, there was some wartime tension at the department level. At any moment investigators might appear to see whether regulations were being carried out, always with the possibility of failure-to-comply due to simple clerical error. But there was no real conflict of purpose, and Nelson's office often reaffirmed that nothing less than affirmative cooperation would do.

Nelson also always responded positively to community war efforts, whether it was a local Red Cross project involving the provision of bandages (Grace led such an effort at the store), the sale of war bonds, or a call for rationing or scrap collection. In October 1942, when the government conducted a drive for scrap metal to use for munitions, Dayton's ordered workmen to the roof of the building on the Eighth Street side to dismantle the great electric sign that, with hundreds of lights, had long written the store's signature on the night sky.

When the war ended, Nelson ran a full-page advertisement printed in January 1946, including this letter:

> As our 44th anniversary rolls around we are thinking of the loyalty of our many friends whose patronage has made the growth of the store possible. As we remind ourselves of your patience during the past few years when we have not been able to show you the merchandise selections and the service [that] you deserve, we want you to know that we are aware of your forbearance.
>
> As for merchandise, we now have lots of it but are still short of a relatively small number of the most important items. Nylons are a matter of a few days more; we have been accumulating them until we have enough . . . electric appliances, barring unforeseen delays, should be in stock sometime in the spring. Also radios. Sheets and other household linens will be in larger quantities sometime in early summer, we hope. More men's clothes and shirts by late summer, cotton and rayon fabrics in large amounts by summer, also lingerie and other cotton garments.
>
> Small quantities are dribbling in. Unless manufacturing is further delayed, production will increase and we will have more. We

will tell you when we do. So, we hope your patience is not quite exhausted. This year should, month by month, make it easier for you to buy and us to sell. Hopefully then, we thank you.

Now that the war was over, normal desires reasserted themselves. Probably no limitation had disturbed the well-groomed American woman more than the inability to obtain "silk" stockings. Dayton's had prepared for this moment with a plan to accumulate enough nylons to make fair distribution among its customers possible. By February 1946, it had 90,000 pairs, enough to justify a sale.

Everyone knew that when stockings went on sale there would be a scramble to get them. Someone suggested Dayton's rent a public building—the Minneapolis Auditorium, perhaps—for the event. But Nelson didn't want the sale to become an athletic event divorced from the store. Dayton's was the provider of necessities and comforts. (While he wasn't comfortable with a PR role for himself, Nelson had a clear, distinct vision for the store.) The sale must take place there.

And so it did. Dayton's made up packages of two pairs each—the limit to a customer—and put them in the sub-basement fur vaults for safekeeping. Customers were to be admitted by the Eighth Street door, take the elevator to the third floor, and line up in a queue making its way by escalator back to the second floor. There the line wound through several departments to the cashiers' windows. With receipt in hand, the customer would continue to the counters where the stockings were stacked by size and price. The sale was, of course, a huge success.

Nelson spoke of the first year after the war with amusement. Ending a talk to the representatives of a 100-plus affiliates of Northwest Bancorporation in Dayton's tearooms, he said, in the idiom of the time: "The year 1946 was wonderful for retail merchants, both in volume and in profits realized. Merchants will look back and talk about it the way the old maid talked about the one time she was kissed."

But Nelson had again built up the reserve account, and he was eager to build on the early postwar boom. In a news release announcing still further expansion, he said:

> The retail business has had a very considerable growth in Minneapolis in recent years, much more than we foresaw. During the war it was not possible to build, so now we must not only catch up with requirements of present volume but [also] prepare for the future, which we regard optimistically.
>
> For nearly 44 years, at frequent intervals, Dayton's has been adding to its plant and keeping it up to date, always with faith in [the city's] future. We still have that faith . . . we see evidence that the city is going to have a postwar growth in industry, business, and population. In that confidence we are preparing to do our share.

The outward signs of this faith were the blueprint drawings, made late in 1945, for expansion of the store to 12 full stories—of all but the original building at Nicollet and Seventh. This meant adding five floors from the corner of Eighth Street to the garage, which needed just two more floors. The expansion added 30 percent more sales area and extended the escalators from the fourth to the seventh floors. The plan included a new delivery building on Olson Memorial Highway and the purchase of a warehouse on Third Avenue South.

The expansion, begun in January 1946, was completed in 1948 for a total cost of $1,550,000. It was the culmination of the vision of George Draper Dayton; his grandson Donald played a major role in seeing it through. Specific improvements included the new Sky Room opened on the eighth floor in 1947, the remodeled Looking Glass salon opened in April 1948, the Oval Room and related shops opened in August 1948, and the enlarged furniture department on the seventh floor opened in February 1949.

While the boom was on, the store was selling in still another climate. Dreams born and nurtured during the war flowered in its wake,

This schematic shows the fulfillment of George's vision for the store.

and Dayton's was happy both to instigate and to make its customers' dreams come true. The Oval Room is a case in point.

In August 1938, Stuart Wells had joined Dayton's as department manager of Women's and Misses' Gowns and Better Dresses. Born in Minneapolis, Wells had taken his taste for design to New York, where after associations with Macy's and Bergdorf Goodman, he established a shop next door to Saks Fifth Avenue. When his father urged him to join the family investment business, Wells returned to Minneapolis but took a job with Young-Quinlan, a fashionable dress store at Nicollet and Ninth Street (today the home of JB Hudson Jewelers), just a block from Dayton's. Owner Elizabeth Quinlan earlier had been a member of the Goodfellow's staff.

When Wells's plans proved more ambitious and innovative than Quinlan cared to sponsor, she said to Nelson, "You take him. Dayton's can afford him." The department store was glad to have him, so much so that some years later Stuart Wells became its first outside-of-the-family Dayton Company president.

The new recruit managed the "better dresses" of the Model Room, its name changed from the French Room because the impending war was already cutting off European style sources. The Model Room gave Wells what he considered to be a job in routine merchandising—not the center of high fashion that he, and Dayton's, desired. So over the next years, Wells collaborated with Nelson and Donald Dayton and key merchandiser Dayne Donovan, to provide a place where the woman of taste could outfit herself from head to toe. Later Wells developed a "trend merchandising" curve to maximize sales and minimize stock.

Striving to do only what they could do "as well as it could be done anywhere," the foursome emulated the best department-store fashion boutique—the 28 Shop of Chicago's Marshall Field's, opened in

Dayton's Sky Room (1949)

Oval Room millinery (August 1948)

1941. Then Dayton's Oval Room evolved from just a new name for the Model Room (April 1943) into the fashion-forward center the executives envisioned. It made Dayton's the 2nd-largest privately owned and the 9th-largest store overall in the 17th-largest city.

The first task in creating the Oval Room was to find sources for the stylish clothes it wanted to sell. Because of its reputation, Dayton's was able to attract designers and manufacturers such as Philip Mangone, Hattie Carnegie, Nettie Rosenstein ("mother of the little black dress"), and the first of all of them, Adrian, a Hollywood designer and painter turned fashion designer. The Adrian collection, inspired by the designer's experience on an African safari, boosted the prestige of the Oval Room when it reopened with oval reception space in August 1948. Salon upon salon provided access to the most fashionable dresses, coats, hats, blouses, skirts, shoes, and accessories for the discerning shopper.

The ads of the Oval Room were printed separately from the larger store's offerings. A new delivery box—longer, wider, and lower—carried Oval Room dresses. The tissue paper protecting the garments in their boxes was Grade A. The bill appeared not on top but in an envelope at the bottom of the box. The impulse for all this was not to exclude but to attract customers, even those "just looking," because one day they might return to buy. At the Oval Room, women of the region could see the shape of things to come.

Because of its high-fashion leadership in the Oval Room, Dayton's moved easily into leadership in high-style medium- and lower-priced clothes as well. The Oval Room kept people style-conscious, with annual style shows, for example, featuring the new collections of American designers. Sometimes Dayton's collaborated in these events with the Friends of the Institute (Minneapolis Institute of Arts) or the Women's Auxiliary of the Hennepin County Medical Association, who used the shows as fundraisers.

Dayton's window display for Easter 1947

With both Nelson's and Donald's approval, the Oval Room began advertising in *Vogue* and *Harper's Bazaar*. The two-page ads used every device of format—camera angle, type, margin, and page orientation—to present the store as distinctive. The bold ads had the desired effect of promoting style in goods sold throughout the store and made Dayton's a nationwide shopping "destination."

Another example of horizontal expansion enlarged on the services of the bridal bureau. Thoughts of the earlier economic depression had clouded new bridal celebrations, and Dayton's had for a long time only one fitting room for brides and their parties. Buying for the bridal trade was dispersed among three specialists in other fields who tended to buy for the department "on the way to the train." But one enterprising staff member analyzed the wedding market at the public

Brides Bureau (August 1948)

library, put together scrapbooks about weddings of every kind, and approached Hugh Arthur with a proposal. He sent her to Nelson, who made her the buyer for Dayton's new Brides Bureau, placed next to what was soon to become the Oval Room.

A litany of other departments and specialties followed: The Interior Decorating Studio, which had existed since the 1920s, partnered with its neighbor, the Hotel Radisson, in 1945 to remodel its penthouse as an attraction for celebrities and others of fine taste. After the war, an Interior Decorating Studio rep began buying items from Europe, providing unique objects through direct buying and thus fine bargains for customers. In 1949 Dayton's opened a new Studio of Interior Decorating and Designing.

Through the 1940s Dayton's moved from its old paternalism to regard its workforce as an asset of business. Making the most of that asset meant giving the individual the best training and opportunity possible, as well as making the employee feel secure in his or her job. Dayton's established the five-and-a-half-day week in 1947, before most others; soon the five-day, 40-hour week and more liberal vacations became the rule.

During the 1940s, as the store and the city grew together, Dayton's participated in almost every aspect of the public life, something Donald tremendously enjoyed. Providing some entertainment of its own, the store persuaded, for example, comedian Bob Hope to serve as commentator at one fashion show, and Ilka Chase, daughter of the longtime editor of *Vogue,* to preside at another—with models from Paris. Dayton's designers created sweepstakes-worthy floats for the city's annual Aquatennial celebration, and store candidates three times became the Aquatennial's "Queen of the Lakes."

The changing order of the 1940s was evident in the retirement of many of the store's longtime executives. On January 31, 1948, three members of the team—vice-presidents John Per-Lee, C. J. Larson, and Hugh Arthur—went out together with these words from Nelson:

Summertime window display featuring the 1950 Minneapolis Aquatennial

"While we rejoice with these men that they can retire . . . they are going to be sorely missed . . . Personally, I have counted heavily on these three the past 25 years and owe them a genuine debt of gratitude." Two years later, on January 31, 1950, came the departure of other trusted executives—A. C. White, W. A. Dillman, H. S. Skinner, and G. L. Larson.

The greatest loss to the store was that of Nelson himself, a generating force in all the company's interests until 1948, when from the outside view he suddenly retired. But he had been ill since 1946. What started as a stubborn cough was ultimately diagnosed as a tumor on his sternum.

With the war ended, Bruce, Wally, Ken, and Doug were released from military service to be home for their father's apparently successful surgery that year. All but Doug, who was finishing his schooling at Amherst, joined the store that year. Bruce resumed his role as treasurer, while Wally and Ken started their careers in the stockroom, Wally moving toward sales support (he became service superintendent early in 1950) and Ken toward merchandising (general merchandising manager early in 1950). Nelson returned to his office and to the daily routine in the store, on the farm, and in civic life. Dayton's sales reached $43 million by the end of 1946—the year it began giving 5 percent of its pretax profits to charity.

All was not good news, however. One day at Boulder Bridge, when Nelson reached out to swat a mosquito, the movement broke his collarbone. The cancer had spread. He called a family conference, and with physician standing by, told Grace and "the boys" the not-so-positive prognosis. In 1947, Nelson named Donald general manager of the store. And he sat for a professional portrait by a leading photographer.

Still Nelson continued his interest in all the concerns of his career. After the last phase of construction was completed in 1948, he visited the new furniture floor one morning in a wheelchair. Eventually, he

Workers in Dayton's appliance department, servicing early television sets

became bedridden—hence his public retirement. Son Bruce kept him informed and in the decision loop, reporting to him often at home in Minneapolis or at Boulder Bridge Farm and conveying his wishes to store executives and employees.

The store continued to grow, to the tune of $60 million in sales annually by the end of 1950. But in January of that year, *The Dayton News* (employee newsletter) published this last note from Nelson—almost a repeat of one he had written the year before:

> During the holidays, it gave me great pleasure to receive Christmas greetings from so many Daytonians. I enjoyed opening the many cards and reading your kind notes. I appreciate deeply your thoughtful consideration of me.
>
> I wish that I could thank each of your personally, but you will realize that that would be impossible for me to do. Therefore I would

Dayton's Oak Grille restaurant, 1949

The Long Pull

Dayton's at Eighth Street and Nicollet Avenue after the 1948 expansion

like to take this opportunity to sincerely thank each of you and to extend to all best wishes for a very Happy New Year.

Sincerely yours,
G. Nelson Dayton

In his last months, Nelson recognized the changing times. Sensing the trend toward a less restrictive Sabbath, he was determined not to leave his sons strapped by the store's policy of no work, no lighted windows, no advertising on Sunday. He removed the prohibition from The Dayton Company bylaws so that his sons would be free to do what they deemed necessary. The restriction of lighting store windows was the first to go (in the 1950s).

Also, wishing to establish Grace in a more comfortable home, Nelson sold their house on Blaisdell Avenue and purchased another at

The Long Pull

1720 Franklin. The new home suited them both in the months before Nelson's death, and Grace enjoyed living there the rest of her life. Later she had a place in Florida too. With Bruce's help, Nelson prepared a new will—to provide Grace greater benefits and their sons a more flexible approach to dividing his remaining estate (see chapter 10).

Nelson conversed regularly with family and friends, many of who stopped by to visit. Wally's wife, Mary Lee Lowe Dayton, particularly remembers visiting Nelson at the home on Franklin with their infant daughter, Sally, to snap a photo of the two. Nelson was also pleased to know Donald's sons Edward and John and Bruce's sons Mark and Brandt as children.

In February 1950 the Community Chest and Council of Hennepin County offered its annual award "for distinguished service in the fields of social work and public welfare" jointly to Nelson and Grace, the first ever to a couple. "You who have worked with them,"

The Dayton home at Franklin and Knox

said their friend Bill Huff in making the award, "know that their unselfishness in giving their time and their knowledge to community affairs has been one of their most generous contributions . . . I know of no civic activity that has been turned away when it sought their help."

Nelson could not be present for the award ceremony; Grace accepted the award, saying: "I know that it is made chiefly on my husband's account." But the community had long since recognized her as one of its most appealing and useful citizens. And the Daytons' talent for collaboration had become an asset to all around them.

That month Nelson was present and still presiding at the annual meeting of the Okabena Company, which probably took place at his bed. About seven weeks later, George Nelson Dayton reached the end of his long pull.

On April 1, 1950, the day Nelson died in the hospital at age 63, the *Minneapolis Star* noted:

> To welfare, religion, and civic enterprise, he gave both his energy and his means, and scores of ventures succeeded because he believed in them. His interest reflected the . . . traits [that] made him so admirable as a family man and friend. With typical foresight he trained his sons and associates to carry on the business [that] bears the family name. He instilled in them his own sense of community responsibility . . . The activities of which he was part will find new leaders, stimulated by the example that he set, but Minneapolis, sorrowing at his passing, acknowledges an immense debt to a preeminent citizen.

In essence, Nelson had done what he could do as well—or better—than it was done anywhere.

Nelson's wife, Grace, and their sons were with him when he died. His funeral two days later was private, but a public memorial service followed at Westminster Presbyterian Church. The store closed in memoriam that day.

Grace Bliss Dayton

9

About Grace

According to all who remember and have written of her, Grace Bliss Dayton was the very embodiment of her name: the most charming and gracious of persons, someone grateful for her blessings and talents and eager to share them. She loved her wide and extended family, she had high moral standards, and she always made others feel welcome and comfortable. She had, according to her granddaughter Lucy, a great sense of humor. And she was "upbeat, always happy to see people. She loved everyone, and she loved entertaining. She had great class."

Upon her marriage to Nelson, Grace immediately fit into the larger Dayton family. She had little respite before, as George Dayton noted, she took "on the burdens and privileges of service." Indeed, over her lifetime, Grace served many civic, social welfare, cultural, religious, and educational institutions and causes.

Grace Bliss wrote of her aunt: "From the beginning, Grace [Bliss Dayton] was a rather advanced wife, moving out into the community earlier in the marriage than was usual for her contemporaries, clearly

Grace

with Nelson's approval. She continued her active participation without interruption for the personal circumstances [pregnancies!] many women would have considered good excuses to ease up."

Grace conducted an American Red Cross clothing drive during World War I, less than five years after she became part of the Dayton family. And when the United States entered the war in 1917, the Minneapolis unit set about equipping and staffing a mobile base hospital that spent most of the war tending to the wounded on the battlefields of France. On the home front, Red Cross volunteers knitted supplies for the soldiers abroad.

Grace was named to the Maternity Hospital's board of directors in 1922, and later she served as president of the organization, later called Ripley Memorial Hospital and still later, the Martha Ripley Foundation.* For various periods, she was president of the Minneapolis Woman's Club and a director of the YWCA and its parallel organization, the Woman's Christian Association, which operated residences for working "girls" and elderly people. She was a director of the Community Chest and United Fund, and from 1935 to 1947 she served on the budget and distribution committee of the Community Chest and Council of Hennepin County. Later she was a member of the steering committee that planned its evolution to the United Fund.

Grace was a trustee of Dakota Wesleyan University, her alma mater in Mitchell, South Dakota. She was also a member of Thursday Musical of Minneapolis, which still offers programs featuring local musicians. She was a member of the advisory board of the Women's Association of the Minneapolis Symphony Orchestra (now the Minnesota Orchestra). She went to its concerts faithfully as well as to Metropolitan Opera performances in Northrop Auditorium at the University of Minnesota.

Grace was a trustee of the Dayton Foundation, and after Nelson's death she was president of the Granelda Foundation, established through Nelson's will. She was throughout her marriage and widowhood an active member of Westminster Presbyterian Church of Minneapolis, and for a period she was president of its Women's Association. She taught both Sunday school and Bible classes at the church for many years. Even before the Daytons spent summers at Boulder Bridge Farm, they rented at Lake Minnetonka, and Grace conducted informal religious services at a nearby YWCA camp for girls.

During World War II, Grace, along with her Minneapolis neighbor Bernice (Mrs. John) Dalrymple, was in charge of sewing in the

---

* The hospital building, now called Ripley Gardens, is used today for affordable housing. Mary Lee Lowe Dayton, Wally's wife, later served with Grace on that board.

Grace Bliss Dayton with her niece Grace Bliss and gentleman unknown

production department for the Hennepin County Chapter of the American Red Cross. Dayton's Department Store provided ample space for the work on its second floor, and volunteers provided the labor. Set up soon after Germany's invasion of its European neighbors, the program concentrated on garments for refugees of all ages. The chapter added items for servicemen after the United States entered the war in 1941.

Grace's niece Grace Bliss, whom the Daytons had supported after her father died, later compiled a Bliss family history detailing some parts of her aunt's life. Of Grace's Red Cross service, she wrote:

> Grace displayed her keen sense of organization in running this operation. She bought materials wholesale and shipped them to local factories [that] donated cutting [services] during slack times. With the help of volunteers, she bundled the cut materials for distribution to women's groups. She maintained contact with the groups to speed the return of finished garments. She inspected the results and, with a few secret volunteers, repaired any unsatisfactory work. Finally, she and her crew packed the completed clothing into bundles of assorted

sizes for shipment to Europe. If this sounds like a full-time job with very little time in a comfortable desk chair, it was that. She worked at it from 9:00 to 5:00, often six days a week, with stunning results.

In six years the unit produced 605,000 garments and articles for soldiers, hospital patients, and refugees. Grace may also have participated in Red Cross efforts such the local Blood Donor Center and Gray Lady or canteen services.

Through her life in Minneapolis, Grace hosted various dinner parties, teas, and receptions for charitable causes, particularly at the Dayton home at 2321 Blaisdell Avenue. She made sure her boys had the social

Grace in the dining room of her home on Franklin Avenue

skills—including dancing—to participate in such events: The Daytons hosted dancing classes for young people in the third-floor ballroom there. Bruce remembers that a Mrs. Higby was the dancing teacher and that he learned enough from her to win a wartime polka contest.

At Boulder Bridge Farm, of course, Grace pursued other interests, especially gardening. She was among the first gardeners in Minnesota to grow azaleas, which she nursed before planting outside, in a special shed built for the purpose. She loved sharing her gardens, and she was a loyal member and president of the Lake Minnetonka Garden Club. She often invited it members to visit her gardens at the farm.

Shortly before Nelson's death in 1950, the Community Chest recognized Grace's devotion to the community in honoring the Daytons with its award for distinguished service, which she accepted on their behalf. Not long after that, Dakota Wesleyan University honored her by naming a new women's residence for her. Grace Bliss Dayton Hall housed 198 women students. The plaque in its lobby reads:

Grace Bliss Dayton Hall
1957
Named in honor of an alumna benefactor of
Dakota Wesleyan University

Grace unveiled the plaque on Homecoming Day, October 18, 1958.

After Nelson's death, Grace handled her life with great dignity, expanding her service to her wider community as well as to her wider family. A member of the Friends of the Institute (Minneapolis Institute of Arts), Grace cochaired the Christmas Festival at the museum in 1953. By that time son Bruce had been a trustee of the institute for several years. Grace greatly enjoyed visiting its museum exhibits, and she often told people, "It's fun there."

In 1957 Grace was cochair, again with Minneapolis neighbor Bernice Dalrymple, of the Women's Division of the Minnesota Centen-

Dakota Weslyn University named a dormitory to honor Grace Bliss Dayton.

nial celebration. And Grace was a member of the board of the United Negro College Fund. Bruce recalls her calling on the first black family moving into the Kenwood area as well as her provision of financial aid for three black students at Blake School for Boys. She was the first—and only—woman of her time to be elected a member of Blake Corporation, which operated the school. All her sons and several of her grandsons were educated there.

Socially, Grace was a member of the Woodhill Country Club, the Minikahda Club, the American Association of University Women, and the National Society of the Colonial Dames of America in the State of Minnesota.

When Minnesota Republican Walter Judd, a physician and former medical missionary, served in Congress in the 1950s and '60s, Grace served in a political capacity: She was one of a small group of advisors with whom he consulted regularly on current political issues. Known

Grace B. Dayton Wildflower Garden

Given Grace's love for and interest in gardening, her five sons concocted a way to both memorialize their mother and carry on that interest. They provided the resources for the design and execution of the Grace B. Dayton Wildflower Garden of the Minnesota Landscape Arboretum at 3675 Arboretum Drive in Chaska.

Wishing a convenient way to research plants suitable for growing in a northern climate, in 1956 the Men's Garden Club of Minneapolis approached the Minnesota State Horticultural Society about founding an arboretum. Two years later, with the help of a gift from the Lake Minnetonka Garden Club (Grace provided funding for an option on the land), 160 acres near the University of Minnesota Fruit Breeding Farm was purchased for the university for such a project.

Grace may have been excited about the development of the arboretum, but her son Bruce remembers that she did not seem particularly excited about the wildflower garden; perhaps she viewed its naming in her honor as ostentatious. At any rate, the Grace B. Dayton Wildflower Garden opened in 1960 as a showcase for endangered native plants of the Upper Midwest. Among the many native blooms there are the dwarf trout lily, the Virginia bluebell, the trillium, the cardinal flower, and Minnesota' state flower, the showy lady slipper. Visitors can find more orchids blooming in the wildflower garden than in any other public outdoor garden in the state.

The extensive garden has undergone major renovations due to a loss of canopy from Dutch elm disease and a violent storm in the 1970s. Today it hosts such events as the mile-long "Youth Daffodil

Dash." The garden has been described as "a calm respite from anything you need respite from, [a place where one can] enjoy soothing sun or breezy shade, with banks of flowers blooming all around, fruits of the spring wildflowers still lingering on their stems, background chatter of songbirds in the trees . . . The stream babbles beneath a patch of cardinal flower."

Arboretum landscape gardener and woody plants specialist Jeff Johnson has called the garden named for Grace "my favorite spot": "The meandering path through trees, shrubs, and forbs is a paradise year round. I feel as if I am in the Garden of Eden. The woodland wildflowers are not matched anywhere I've seen."

Surely Grace would be pleased to know how the area is enjoyed today.

for his strong conservative stance on China, Judd took a more moderate stance on social issues, perhaps due to Grace's influence.

Finally, in 1961 Grace was elected at age 71 to a three-year term on the board of the Career Clinic for Mature Women in Minneapolis.

In Grace's public deeds, wrote her niece, she displayed "high intelligence, great energy, unusual generosity with time and thought, as well as gifts, and a strong humanitarian bent. Her private acts of generosity, kindness, and sympathy were continuous and displayed sensitivity to individual interests and needs." Grace Bliss (the younger) listed several occasions prompting expressions of her aunt's compassion: Seeing unemployed, homeless men lined up at a soup kitchen in the early 1930s, for example, Grace noticed the details: they did have "warm coats and sturdy shoes, at least."

Grace with her stepmother, Addie Corliss Bliss

Always aware that others might lack the family and home comforts that she enjoyed, Grace remembered former household employees with cheerfully hand-wrapped, useful holiday gifts. And when she could not visit an elderly nurse who had helped care for members of her family, she asked her niece to do so for her.

Grace made a point of knowing something about the people she would be meeting at her own and others' dinner parties and events. If the guest of honor was from another country, for example, she learned about his or her homeland before meeting. As a result, Grace was a great conversationalist and a preferred dinner guest.

Her eagerness to learn about and experience other cultures also rendered her an enthusiastic traveler, though once, in Japan, her interest resulted in the consumption of roasted sparrows and fried baby bumble bees. She ate enough to keep the host happy.

Grace traveled little before the 1950s. Particularly during the last few years of Nelson's illness, she took care of everything for him, planning and arranging visits from family and friends in town or at Boulder Bridge Farm. Even before he was ill, however, Nelson had not liked travel—he chose trains over planes—and while Grace accompanied him to other states when he had to go away, they never went overseas together. She did go once on her own—to visit the flower shows in Holland.

After Nelson's death, Grace toured other countries on a regular basis, frequently with Oscar Webber, whose brother, Dick, owned 51 percent of Hudson's Department Store of Detroit. As mentioned earlier, the Webber brothers matched Draper and Nelson Dayton in age and had been good friends of the Daytons for years.

Grace Dayton and Oscar Webber, who had also lost his spouse, enjoyed each other very much and once discussed marriage. Neither wished to leave their homes and families in Minneapolis and Detroit, however, so they remained friends who often traveled the world together—mainly Asia and Europe. One itinerary, for a Mediterranean

RMA CARONIA MEDITERRANEAN CRUISE - 1960
MR. OSCAR WEBBER AND MRS. GRACE B. DAYTON

Confirming our telephone conversation of today, I am detailing below proposed arrangements for Mr. Webber and Mrs. Dayton.

The following regular shore excursions are confirmed: Tours 1A, 7, 9, 10, 11, 13, 22, 32, 36, 39, 40, 42B, 56 and 58. Cost per person $644.

The supplement for exclusive use of the vehicles on tours in Morocco, Malta and Naples are as follows: Tour 7, $70.00; Tour 9, $5.00; Tour 42B, $11.00.

The following private cars are tentatively reserved:

Istanbul	Including courier, entrance fees, lunch with tour members at Hilton Hotel.	
	Per Person	$21.00
Haifa	Including English-speaking driver for Nazareth only.	
	Per Person	$21.00
Athens	Including guide, entrance fees and lunch at Grande Bretagne.	
	Per Person	$26.00
Barcelona	Including guide, entrance fees and lunch at Montserrat.	
	Per Person	$19.50
Palma	Including guide.	
	Per Person	$17.00
Malaga	Including guide and trip to Granada only.	
	Per Person	$35.00
	Total Per Person	$139.50

It is naturally understood that this per person price is based on two persons being in the car.

Standard tours by motor coach, which roughly parallel the above private car arrangements, would be the following tours; Tours 14, 24, 28, 49, 53 and 55, and would come to $75.50 per person.

The first page of Grace and Oscar's Mediterranean cruise itinerary

```
               SHORE PROGRAM - MR. WEBBER & MRS. DAYTON.
               --------------------------------------------

                                    Mr. Webber              Mrs. Dayton

                        Group       $206.00                 $206.00

                        0-15          16.50                   16.50
                        0-17          12.00                   12.00
                        0-19          11.00                   11.00
                        0-20           3.00                    3.00
                        0-26         114.00                  114.00
                        0-29         138.00                  138.00
                        0-32          11.00                   11.00
                        0-33          14.00                   14.00
                        0-34           3.00                    3.00
                        0-35          24.00                   24.00
                        0-36          15.00                   15.00
Special     Taupo       Car          456.00
            Hobart      Car           27.00
            Hobart/Melb. Air          20.70          Air      20.70
            Melbourne   Transfer      27.75          Car      50.00
            Melb./Sydney Car         353.00          Car      45.00

                        Total      $1,451.95        Total   $683.20
                                   -----------              ---------
```

Tour 26 - (private BUICK with driver
  including two singles w/shower at
  LAKE Hotel, Taupo, Mon. Feb. 10) -
  including tips and driver's bed/board $456.00

Hobart - (private auto with driver,
  including tips, from ship's arrival
  to airport departure) - Sun. Feb. 16   27.00

Hobart/Melbourne Air tickets -
  (ANA Flight 156 - dep. 4:30 p.m.)   20.70 $20.70

Melbourne - transfer Airport/Hotel on
  arrival, plus Single with bath at
  Hotel AUSTRALIA Sun. Feb. 16 and
  Mon. Feb. 17   27.75

Melbourne - Single with bath at Hotel
  AUSTRALIA Sun. Feb. 16 and Mon. Feb.17
  plus private auto full-day Mon. Feb.17
  including tips   50.00

Tour 29* (private DE SOTO with driver through
  out, including tips and driver's bed/board) 353.00

Sydney - private auto to Blue Mountains
  Fri. Feb. 21, including tips   _____   45.00

                            Total $884.45 $115.70
                                             ---------   --------

Page 2 shows that Oscar usually paid for the car.

cruise on Cunard's *Caronia* in 1960, lists shore excursions at six ports: Istanbul, Haifa, Athens, Barcelona, Palma, and Malaga. Each excursion included transportation by private automobile. The itinerary (see pages 192–93) indicates that Grace and Oscar split exactly the cost of the excursions except that Mr. Webber usually paid for the car.

Sometimes Grace's family saw her off (this was the day of on-ship "Bon Voyage" parties) from New York or other port cities. Often one son or another, or the sons together, sent her flowers, sometimes a beautiful plant from which she could cut a fresh corsage to wear on her dinner dress every evening. She wrote letters to relatives at home thanking them and telling them about her travels and arrival/departure dates. They sent her telegrams and birthday letters and gifts.

Much of Grace's worldwide travel was by ocean liner, but Mary Lee Lowe Dayton also remembers Grace going to Alaska by plane, "sitting in her seat with her hat on." As she had done with her boys, Grace took the grandchildren and their mothers on vacations by car, particularly to Mitchell, the Black Hills, and other places in South Dakota.

Despite her interest in Minneapolis and the world, Grace's greatest passion was her more immediate and growing family. She attended faithfully the activities of her sons, such as Bruce's riding events. And Bruce remembers Grace falling to her knees in tears after one of his brother left for the war.

Grace's in-laws, both older and eventually younger, all considered her a good match for Nelson, and all came to love her dearly for herself. Everyone called her "Mother." Her son Bruce remembers walking with his mother from their home at 2321 Blaisdell to visit his grandfather George Dayton's house at 2020 Blaisdell one day. Before they left, he heard George tell Grace how much he loved her and that after his wife, Emma, he had most loved and appreciated *her*.

Son Wally's wife, Mary Lee Lowe Dayton, remembers Grace as "wonderful, friendly, sweet, beautiful, and very caring." She recalls

Ken Dayton recalled his mother taking the boys to see Potato Creek Johnny (above from a news clipping), who taught them how to pan for gold.

that Grace went to New York every fall to visit her niece Grace Bliss, who would come to stay with Grace at her hotel. Often they would go sightseeing or shopping (Grace was always beautifully dressed) together. And if Grace happened to be in New York when Wally and Mary Lee were there on business, Grace and Mary Lee always had lunch together.

Says Mary Lee, "We had both married into wealth, and we had given some thought to being well known, about what the difficulties are and how do you deal with them. My father was a minister too. So we had some things in common, and Grace and I enjoyed talking with each other."

Mary Lee had been a recipient of the Dayton Foundation long before she dated Wally: "When I applied for Vassar," she said, "it was a big deal—and the Dayton Foundation paid for it. I have a brother seven years younger, and later Wally and I sent him to Princeton, then to the University of Minnesota School of Medicine."

Mary Lee's father, Arnold Lowe, who was a minister of Westminster Presbyterian Church, "knew people at the forefront, and he used to give lectures on current theological thinking. Once Grace commented to me upon hearing another clergyman speak: "It's a good thing your father isn't alive—he wouldn't want to hear that modern interpretation."

"Grace adored her grandchildren," says Mary Lee, "and she was thrilled to have some girls in the family." (Wally and Mary Lee had

Grace hosting a party for her grandchildren

Bruce and his family on their way to Sunday lunch at Grace's house

four daughters, including twins.) Grace loved overnights with the girls at her home on Franklin Avenue. She always had upstairs maid Nellie there to help us."

Mary Lee recalls: "We all had to be on our best behavior—we even had fingerbowls—at her Sunday lunches [or suppers], not every week, but often. The children adored her; they loved going up in the attic with her in the house on Franklin. She was happy."

A five-year-old guest at Franklin Avenue once said, "Great-aunt Grace gave me one of those tall things to drink out of because she knew what a big girl I am.'" She was so pleased that her aunt had "trusted her to manage a goblet."

Grace's granddaughter Lucy recalls crafting in first or second grade a rather crude bunny of clay for her grandmother. The bunny had a lot on holes in which Lucy planted chia. When Lucy presented he gift,

Grace declared it lovely and set it on the table amid her best china. For some time, Lucy found it in Grace's living room whenever she visited there. Lucy also loved the little pool inside that house—and the elevator Grace had put in.

Grace mixed her indulgence of the little ones with *some* discipline: Wally's youngest daughter, Betsy, at about age three, was sitting in a high chair at Sunday lunch. She wanted to leave before the meal was over; that would have been fine, but she refused to ask to be excused. "Please ask Grandmother Dayton to be excused," her mother, Mary Lee, asked several times. Grace supported her daughter-in-law's parental prerogative, so Betsy sat there a long time.

"Cookies were always at hand for the grandchildren," noted niece Grace. But Grace was as thoughtful of the adult members of her family: "Steak and shrimp cocktails graced the menu when grandsons and daughter-in-laws who fancied these items came to dinner."

Grace celebrated Christmas with her family during the 1960s. Nelson often referred to the Earl of Ripon in the classic portrait above as "your boyfriend."

Grace with Presbyterian minister Arnold Lowe and his daughter, Mary Lee

As for Grace's friends, Mary Lee remembers, her mother-in-law treated them all with fond consideration. When Grace went to a meeting or on an outing, she rode in a chauffeured car, but she and the driver usually stopped by or went out of their way to pick up friends or relatives going to the same events. "Even before Nelson died," says Mary Lee, "Grace often came to see us in Deep Haven by herself."

One day Grace told those she was picking up that it would be the last time. And not long after that, Grace Bliss Dayton died at home, surrounded by her sons and other loved ones, 16 years after Nelson, from breast cancer at age 76 on April 1, 1966.

The *Minneapolis Star* noted: "Family and friends remember Mrs. Dayton as a creative gardener, an untiring music lover, a daredevil horsewoman, and a woman who always was modest about her accomplishments." Others remembered her as "the best Bible teacher ever."

A week after her death, on Thursday, April 7, Grace's will was filed with the Hennepin County Probate Court. The will reflects her wide range of interests and service as well as her affection and concern for those who served her long and well.

She left $540,000 to 13 charities, educational institutions, and churches. Her largest bequest, of $250,000, was payable over 20 years to the Granelda Foundation. Other charitable gifts included $50,000 each to the Minneapolis Society of Fine Arts, the Minnesota Orchestral Association, Dakota Wesleyan University, and the University of Minnesota Medical School for Cancer Research. She left $20,000 to the Northwest Hospital Radiation Therapy Teaching and Research Fund and gifts of $10,000 each to the Minnesota Medical Foundation for scholarships, the University of Minnesota School of Nursing Foundation (of which she was a founding member), the YMCA in Minneapolis, Blake School, the Northrop Collegiate School, and the Westminster Presbyterian Church Women's Associations for Missions. And she left a Gauguin woodcut and a Renoir lithograph—*The Hat Pin*—to the Minneapolis Institute of Arts.

Grace at a New Year's dance with her sons and their wives

An oil portrait of Grace

Grace also left $122,000 in bequests ranging from $2,000 to $25,000 to 24 relatives, friends, employees, and former employees, some established as trusts to provide lifetime income. The remainder of her estate, expected to be much less than her charitable giving, went to separate trusts for her five sons, whom she named as executors of her estate. Upon the sale of her estate, they gave many valuable pieces of furniture, porcelain, and art to the Governor's Residence in St. Paul, where her grandson Mark Dayton now resides.

At the time Grace died, she had 16 grandchildren and 2 great-grandchildren. Son Ken said simply, many years later, "We all adored her."

Nelson Dayton

10

Legacy

More than one of Nelson Dayton's sons has noted that Nelson inherited the twinkle in his mother's eye. He passed that and many other blessings along to Grace, to his five sons (which got the twinkle is up for debate), and to the world.

The will of Nelson Dayton demonstrated his trust in his five sons even in its making. Sometime in the four years preceding Nelson's death, son Bruce suggested contacting Goldman Sachs of New York for the recommendation of an estate attorney to help improve the terms of Nelson's will, especially in regard to their mother. James Hemphill, the area representative of Goldman Sachs, suggested Bruce call on Edward McDermott of McDermott Will & Emery of Chicago. McDermoot agreed to visit Nelson in Minneapolis.

When McDermott arrived, he talked with all of the Dayton brothers before going with Bruce to visit Nelson at his home. There the three discussed the distribution of Nelson's estate. McDermott Will & Emory then wrote for Nelson a new will, meant to provide more for his widow. The will was flexible, granting percentages of the estate to Grace and to her five sons. Bruce was to figure out the particular assets later. In the meantime, he suggested recapitalizing and dividing the equity of Dayton's (again) into preferred and common stock.

All the Dayton boys were present when Nelson died from cancer at age 63, and each was already part of The Dayton Company. Its only asset then was Dayton's Department Store, founded by their grandfather George Draper Dayton, in downtown Minneapolis early in 1902. Nelson, the store's general manager from 1923 to 1947, had bought out most of the common-stock owners and turned down opportunities to sell the store, wishing to keep it for his sons. Each of the brothers had purchased part of the common stock he owned. Each borrowed $100,000 to do so.

As the reader may recall, all the brothers had more or less begun in Dayton's receiving room, learning how the merchandise came in, then following it from stock room to sales floor. The four younger brothers were discharged from military service or called home from college when Nelson had surgery in 1946. All worked full time at the store at least during the last two years of Nelson's illness. Donald, the oldest brother, was the general manager.

After Nelson died, Bruce listed the assets of the estate, methodically coming up with a plan that all agreed was generous and fair. Several months later, the settlement was complete. Most of Nelson's estate, including a large block of the newly issued, preferred stock (paying a comfortable dividend) went to their mother, Grace. The five Dayton boys each inherited $125,000 and one-fifth of the controlling common stock of the company.

Added to what they already had, the inheritance gave the five brothers about 90 percent of the common stock—absolute control of the store and its growth. Thus Nelson provided his five sons with little cash but huge opportunity to profit from the future growth of the business. Little did they then realize where that might lead.

Legacy

As the reader may also recall, Nelson left his sons with something greater—the legacy of advice and example in his admonition to "do only what you can do as well as it can be done anywhere."

He had shown them the way in his ethical leadership of Dayton's Department Store, making money every year and, even during the Great Depression, paying the same dividend. (See chart of the store's growth in sales/profit on pages 206–207). He had also shown the way in his management of Boulder Bridge Farm, improving the Guernsey stock in Minnesota to the point that in 1950, the year of the farm's sale, his livestock had won more grand national championships that any other to date, and more than half of the Guernseys competing at the Minnesota State Fair were descended from Boulder Bridge stock.

So, in 1950, the five brothers—Don, Bruce, Wally, Ken, and Doug—inherited from their father, George Nelson Dayton, equal shares of the controlling block of common stock of The Dayton Company. At the time, Sears, Roebuck was 40 times larger than Dayton's, and Federated Department Stores was more than 7 times its size. The Dayton brothers over the next three decades turned their single department store (with a branch at the University of Minnesota) into what became the nation's second largest discount retail operation. Double the size of Federated and May stores and larger than Sears/Kmart combined, Target is today the nation's fourth-largest retailer.*

The brothers did so together through expanding west first with the purchase of Fantle's in Sioux Falls, South Dakota, south with a new store in Rochester, Minnesota, and most visibly with the development of Edina's Southdale, then of Rosedale, Brookdale, Ridgedale, and specialties like B. Dalton Books, through merger with Hudson's and the purchase of Mervyn's and Marshall Field's, and finally with the emergence of Target as the lead corporate entity.

Important to Grace was that the brothers accomplish such without rancor. She told her sons they couldn't possibly be in business together

---

* Only Wal-Mart, Home Depot, and Costco sell more.

The Dayton Company Bottom Line

Year	Sales/Revenues	Net Income/Earnings
1902	$ 600,000	
1903	789,253	
1904	847,837	
1905	943,787	
1906	1,219,506	$ 45,081
1907	1,318,498	77,059
1909	1,470,905	69,971
1910	1,981,540	109,253
1911	2,228,131	82,377
1912	2,577,707	184,621
1913	3,261,057	233,281
1914	3,763,292	264,772
1915	4,337,127	369,561
1916	5,021,285	532,850
1917	5,597,137	487,967
1918	6,612,345	280,236
1919	9,543,908	930,510
1920	11,363,213	659,766
1921	11,108,110	645,343
1922	11,636,347	1,665,210
1923	12,212,416	1,109,516
1924	12,794,964	746,936
1925	13,795,677	1,009,996
1926	14,439,971	904,883
1927	15,284,270	914,142
1928	15,939,796	762,337
1929	17,515,577	1,144,022
1930	17,854,287	970,932

The Dayton Company Bottom Line *(continued)*

Year	Sales/Revenues	Net Income/Earnings
1931	16,687,633	539,737
1932	13,250,588	436,249
1933	12,713,366	455,760
1934	13,816,180	590,751
1935	14,864,826	767,047
1936	16,415,930	1,144,603
1937	17,346,625	895,598
1938	17,328,810	882,683
1941	19,991,696	1,156,906
1942	22,463,642	917,940
1943	27,038,813	1,124,314
1944	30,548,015	1,174,221
1945	35,137,438	1,617,429
1946	43,910,740	2,791,522
1947	50,827,235	2,946,937
1948	55,533,887	2,686,507
1949	56,830,315	1,886,691
1950	60,075,763	2,580,749

Dayton's 1950

Five brothers and a cousin (l-r): Bruce, cousin George II, Ken, Doug, Wally, and Don Dayton at the opening of Southdale

without disagreements, "but for heaven's sake, sit down and settle them; don't let them come between you." So they developed a way of working together, not necessarily in harmony on every issue but with a habit of thorough discussion, voting if necessary, and never looking back. Grace celebrated one of her sons' first major business accomplishments by bringing all her grandchildren to the 1956 grand opening of Southdale.

Mary Lee Lowe Dayton speaks highly of the brothers' affection for one another and their ability to work together, of their complementary skills and interests. "They took pride in their family," she says. Brother Ken, now deceased, summed it up: "Perhaps our egos and ambitions didn't stand in the way of doing the right thing in a timely way." Other corporate families were amazed at how well the brothers got along, as well as at what they accomplished.

In 1955 Grace Dayton and others members of the family donated two stained-glass windows to Westminster Presbyterian Church in memory of George Nelson Dayton and his parents. *The Glory*, erected in Nelson's honor on the courtyard side (on the left when facing the narthex) is detailed in the book *Westminster: The Art of a Building,* published by the church in 1997. *The Glory* features a huge center medallion window depicting the compassionate Christ, arms outstretched to all humanity. An outer circle of eight smaller medallions—*The Wonder of Creation*—depicts wind, day and night, mountains and hills, green things, whale, fowl, beasts, and sun, moon, and stars.

The beautiful stained-glass rose window honoring Nelson, as well his designation of 10 percent of his estate to the Granelda Foundation,

The Glory *and* The Wonder of Creation, *in memory of Nelson*

might stand for his legacy of generosity and commitment to community, religious and otherwise. Inherited from those who went before him, Nelson's example of responsible philanthropy—in fulfillment of his belief that "from those to whom much has been given, much is required"—surely influenced the path of his sons.

As the leaders of Dayton's Department Store, then The Dayton Corporation, then Dayton Hudson Corporation (DHC), the brothers continued Nelson's practice, initiated in 1946, of donating 5 percent of pretax corporate earnings, the maximum allowed for deduction for charitable purposes. Many of the foundation's early grants funded the brothers' personal interests—Sister Kenny and hospitals, arts and music organizations, conservation, and the YMCA—as well public welfare entities such as the Community Fund (later United Way). This in the belief that, as Donald said, "Our profitability . . . is as much reliant, if not more reliant, on the quality of life [that] exists there, than on our merchandising and management practices."

The Dayton Foundation remained in the family, the boys serving as well on its board. In 1969, the year that The Dayton Corporation's giving and the Dayton Foundation merged into the Dayton Hudson Foundation, 25 percent of the assets of the Dayton Foundation went to the Minneapolis Foundation for the benefit of United Theological Seminary—to fulfill George's commitment to the missions. The Dayton Hudson Foundation continued to give away 5 percent of its pretax income, grants roughly apportioned 40 percent to social/welfare causes, 40 percent to arts and culture, and 20 percent to miscellaneous philanthropies.

Responsibility to DHC's communities reached beyond financial support, extending to issues of consumerism, affirmative action, and environmental and community development. Performance on matters of social responsibility determined about 5 percent of managerial incentive compensation. In 1976 DHC's giving inspired the Minneapolis Chamber of Commerce to establish the Five Percent Club, soon with

23 members. By 2007 the emerging Keystone Club had 214 members, 134 donating at the 5 percent level, the others giving away 2 percent of their pretax profits. Some came to think of the continuing penchant for Twin Cities corporate giving as "the Minnesota standard."

After the Dayton brothers left management and governance, the corporation's giving practices continued in much the same form until DHC became Target Corporation. According to Laysha Ward of Target, it remains committed to 5 percent giving and the same major funding categories, though some grants and programs now reflect Target's status as a national merchandiser (for instance, in grants to refurbish the Washington National Monument) and to a greater degree the local communities of stores across the country (and now Canada). In 2012 Target gave away $4 million every week.

In a variety of ways beyond corporate giving, the brothers played out the interests and values of Nelson and Grace:

Donald—general manager from 1947, the chief executive of Dayton's until 1965, chair of the board until 1968, and a director until 1977—played a major role in the development of Nicollet Mall in downtown Minneapolis. After retirement, he lived in Florida, still devoting time to Minnesota causes including the Sister Kenny Rehabilitation Institute—whose founder developed a treatment for polio—and Abbot Northwestern Hospital. A member of the National Alliance of Businessmen, the Urban Coalition, and the Twin Cities Metropolitan Council, Donald died in 1989.

Wallace, the middle brother, brought countless efficiencies to the operations area, important to Dayton's growing number of stores. Named president of the Dayton Development Company in 1963, he continued as a vice president of The Dayton Company. Inspired by years of bird watching with his mother and a backpacking expedition into the Alaska wilderness, he left at the end of 1968 to devote his life to wilderness conservation. Continuing on the DHC board until 1977, he became chair of the board of the Nature Conservancy and headed its Minnesota chapter. He chaired the Yellowstone Library Museum Association and was a director of the National Audubon Society, the Wilderness Society, World Wildlife Fund, and Sierra Club Foundation. Three colleges including his alma mater (Amherst) awarded him honorary doctorates before his death in 2002.

After developing a Dayton's store in Rochester, Minnesota, and serving as the first president of Target, then as senior vice president of the DHC, Douglas, the youngest, left the executive ranks in 1971 to start a development capital firm, Dade, Inc. He continued as a DHC director, also until 1977, while also serving his favorite charity—the Minneapolis YMCA (also a favorite of his grandfather George and of his brother Wallace)—particularly as general board chair, as a key leader in pivotal capital campaigns, and as a driving force behind the Y's urban youth work. Doug died on July 6, 2013.

Bruce Dayton, the second oldest brother, replaced Donald as president of Dayton's in 1965, was CEO of Dayton Corporation in 1967 and chair in 1968. He turned the chairmanship over to Ken in 1976, remaining on the board until 1983. Basically he acted as treasurer for all his 43 corporate years. He continued his interest in the Minneapolis Institute of Arts and has been an active donor and trustee for 70 years. Other board service included the Great Minneapolis Metropolitan Housing Corporation, the Brookings Institution, and Honeywell. The University of Minnesota awarded Bruce an honorary doctorate of law in 2005, citing him "a model of ethical and community-minded corporate leadership." He lives in Minnesota.

Kenneth Dayton, the second youngest and an excellent merchandiser, became an even more excellent executive. President of DHC in 1969, he became its CEO in 1970. Known for his advocacy of professional management, organizational surplus, and leadership in the Minneapolis business community, he worked with others to create the Urban Coalition to study causes and recommend solutions when riots broke out in inner-city neighborhoods in the late 1960s. He took the lead on right governance, convinced it was the best way to assure the vitality of the company after the Daytons were gone. He relinquished the title of CEO after six years, having presented the board annually with plans and a timetable for the transition of control to non-family management. The transition was complete in September 1976, when he became chair. A year later he stepped down again, to serve as a director until 1983. Thereafter he devoted much of his time to his longtime favorite cause—the Minnesota Orchestra. Ken died in 2003.

Grace, with (clockwise from left) Donald and his wife Lucy, Ken, Doug, Wally, and Bruce

Nelson surely would have been pleased to know that his sons realized early that the department store was a dying breed of cat, that they grew the business as well as it could be done anywhere, and that they all got out of the way of its growing further. He would have been pleased that they worked without rancor, discussing issues in open-minded fashion until, almost always, they agreed on how to proceed. He would have delighted in their commitment to community and their individual devotion to the causes each most believed in.

Likely he and Grace would have considered their sons their most important, lasting legacy.

Descendants
of
G. Nelson Dayton and Grace Crothers Bliss Dayton
(3 Aug 1886–1 Apr 1950)   (15 Feb 1890–1 Apr 1966)

DONALD CHADWICK (13 Aug 1914–22 Jun 1989) married on 5 Aug 1937 Margaret Jackson (30 Oct 1915–21 Feb 2002):
1. Edward N. (Ned) (b. 10 May 1940)
2. Robert J. (b. 4 Feb 1942)
3. John W. (b. 11 Aug 1945)

ELIZABETH (24 May 1915–24 May 1915)

BRUCE BLISS (b. 16 Aug 1918) married on 21 Jun 1944 Gwendolyn Brandt (12 Jul 1920–), (div.):
1. Mark Brandt (b. 26 Jan 1947)
2. Brandt N. (b. 16 Jun 1949)
3. Lucy B. (O'Keefe) (b. 21 Sep 1950)
4. Anne (Buxton) (b. 29 Sep 1954)

WALLACE CORLISS (12 Mar 1921–27 Oct 2002) married on 15 Oct 1948 Mary Lee Lowe (b. 12 Jun 1925):
1. Sally (Clement) (b. 5 Oct 1949)
2. Katherine (Nielsen) (b. 30 Apr 1951) (twin)
3. Ellen (Sturgis) (b. 30 Apr 1951) (twin)
4. Elizabeth (Dovydenas) (b. 29 Nov 1952)

KENNETH NELSON (20 Jul 1922–19 Jul 2003) married on 12 Jun 1953 Julia Davis Winton (b. 26 Apr 1927)
1. Judson McDonald (23 Oct 1957)
2. Duncan Nelson (28 Apr 1959)

DOUGLAS JAMES (2 Dec 1924–6 Jul 2013) married on 30 Dec 1952 Mary J. Haldeman (12 Apr 1927–30 Aug 2008), div.:
1. David D. (b. 13 Sep 1954)
2. Steven J. (b. 7 Dec 1956)
3. Bruce C. (b. 24 Oct 1959)

Sources

While Bruce Dayton's memories comprise much of this work, the following sources have put dates to and enriched the story of G. Nelson Dayton and his family. The authors drew heavily for stories of Nelson's early life from the research for and content of Bruce Dayton's *George Draper Dayton: A Man of Parts*, for information about Boulder Bridge Farm from his book by that name (as well as from an article by Harry Woodworth in the September 1938 *Golfer and Sportsman*), and for the careers of Nelson's five sons on *The Birth of Target* (see below).

Family Publications

Blair, David Dayton, compiler (materials and information collected by Caroline Dayton Hayden). *Emma Willard Chadwick Dayton: A Genealogical Survey*, Vol. 1. N.c.: Privately published, 1992.

Dayton, Bruce B. "From 10th Street, Worthington to the Nicollet Mall." Typescript speech presented to Worthington High School and Worthington Chamber of Commerce on November 15, 1979.

Dayton, Bruce B. [with Deborah Morse-Kahn]. *Boulder Bridge Farm: As It Was 1926–1950*. [Minneapolis]: Privately published, 2004.

Dayton, Bruce B., and Ellen B. Green. *George Draper Dayton: A Man of Parts*. Minneapolis: Privately published, 1997.

Dayton, Bruce B., with Ellen B. Green. *The Birth of Target*. Minneapolis: Privately published, 2008.

Dayton, Edson C. *A Dayton Genealogy and Biography: The Record of a Family Descent from Ralph Dayton and Alice (Goldhatch) Tritton, Married June 16, 1617, Ashford, County Kent, England (A Genealogical and Biographical Account of One Branch of the Dayton Family in America)*. Hartford, CT: Privately published, 1931. (© 1931 by Caroline K. Dayton, No. 58 of 150 copies presented to Bruce Bliss Dayton by George Draper Dayton, June 7, 1931.)

Dayton Foundation. Statement of the circumstances leading to the creation and endowment of the foundation, signed by members of the Dayton family on January 12, 1920.

Dayton, Emma Willard Chadwick, and George Draper Dayton. *David Draper Dayton.* [Minneapolis]: Privately printed, [1923].

Dayton, George Draper II, as told to Judith Vick. *Our Story: George Draper Dayton II.* Wayzata, MN: Privately published, 1987

Dayton, George Draper, comp. *Emma Willard Chadwick Dayton.* [Minneapolis]: Privately printed after her death in January 1931.

Dayton, George Draper. *An Autobiography.* [Minneapolis]: Privately printed, 1933/34.

Other Family Sources

Selections from letters include those of Emma Dayton to G. Nelson Dayton; George Draper to his children—D. Draper, G. Nelson, Caroline, and Josephine—and their families, and to store employees; G. Nelson to his sons Donald, Bruce, Wallace, Kenneth, and Douglas, as noted in the text. Various family scrapbooks, journals, lettters to and from business and other associates in family archives also informed the work.

Colleen Stauber was helpful in providing access to materials held at Okabena Company, Minneapolis.

Dean Schuenke of Bliss and Company assisted in tracking down family-tree informations and in myriad other ways.

Interviews with Mary Lee Lowe (Mrs. Wallace) Dayton, Julia (Judy) Winton (Mrs. Kenneth) Dayton, and Lucy Bliss Dayton O'Keefe (also a source for photos), as well as an earlier interview with Douglas Dayton enriched the story of Grace Bliss Dayton.

Other Printed Sources

Gray, James. *You Can Get It at Dayton's.* Minneapolis: Privately printed, 1962. (Somewhat unreliable in its facts, this source is nevertheless useful for its color of the times.)

[Kidder, William A.?] "The Dayton Planes." Typescript copy in possession of Bruce Bliss Dayton.)

Rattray, Jeannette Edward. *East Hampton History and Genealogies.* East Hampton, Long Island, NY: (Printed and bound at Country Life Press, Garden City, NY), 1953.

Rose, Arthur P. *An Illustrated History of Nobles County, Minnesota.* Worthington, MN: Northern History, 1908.

Other Sources

Dakota Wesleyan University, Mitchell, SD: Archivist Laurie Langland provided information on Grace Bliss Dayton's graduation and attendance at the dedication of Grace Bliss Dayton Hall.

Internet: Dayton executive obituaries and information, updates on Target Corporation.

Minnesota Historical Society: *Worthington Advance,* 1881–1902, and *Worthington Globe,* 1890–1899, in microfilm editions.

Minnesota Landscape Arboretum, Chanhassen, MN: Barbara Ann DeGroot provided information on the Grace Bliss Dayton Wildflower Garden.

Target Corporation Archive: annual reports, executive speeches, articles from Dayton's employee newletters *DaytonNews* and *Daytonian* and other employee and executive communications, news clippings *(Minneapolis Journal, Minneapolis Star, Minneapolis Times, Minneapolis Tribune,* and various other Minnesota newspapers), and magazine articles about Dayton Company people and events. Archivist Tony Jahn lent much valued assistance.

Westminster Presbyterian Church of Minneapolis: Early conversations with Eloise Hjelmstad and later with Rodney Allen Schwartz, director of the Westminster Gallery & Archive, provided information on Nelson Dayton's family membership and participation in church activities and events and on the memorial windows.

Illustration Credits

Photographs and other illustrations unless otherwise noted are from Dayton family archives (including materials in possession of family members and/or Okabena Corporation) and family publications: pp. 2, 4, 6, 9, 14, 18, 23, 25, 32 top, 34, 36, 40–41, 43, 49, 57, 64, 66, 74, 84 both, 94 (September 1938 *Golfer and Sportsman*), 96–105, 107 top, 108, 112, 114–17, 119–20, 122, 125–27, 129, 131, 133–34, 137, 158, 168, 182, 185, 190, 192–93, 195–201, 213; from James Gray, *You Can Get it at Dayton's:* dust jacket, frontispiece, pp. 16, 29, , 69–70, 178, 205, 208

Other illustrations, listed below are published by permission:

Courtesy of Dakota Wesleyan University Archives, Mitchell, South Dakota: pp. 27 both, 187

Courtesy of Hennepin History Museum, Minneapolis: pp. 110, 146, 148–49, 152

Courtesy of Minnesota Historical Society, St. Paul: pp. 180, 184

Courtesy of Minnesota Landscape Arboretum, Chanhassen: p. 189

Courtesy of Target Corporation: pp. 7, 32 bottom, 35, 37–38, 45, 51, 52 both, 55 both, 58, 62, 67, 68 both, 72, 77, 79–80, 82 both, 85–86, 91, 107 bottom, 160, 162, 169–72, 174–77, 202, 207

Courtesy of Westminster Presbyterian Church, Minneapolis: pp. 142, 209

Index

Page numbers in italics indicate illustrations.

Abraham & Straus, Brooklyn, 46
Allied Stores Corp., 78
American Guernsey Breeders' Journal, 118
American Guernsey Cattle Club, 106
Anderson, Maud Case, 8, 11
Anderson, Sydney, 149
Anoka County, 22
Arey, Hugh (Dr.), 103
Arnold, Ray, 69
Arthur, Hugh, *70*; 44, 47, 65, 70, 161, 173
Associated Merchandising Corp. (AMC), 46–47, 76, 81, 126

B. Dalton Books, 205
B. Forman, advertisement, 81
Bank of Worthington, *9, 14*; 4, 9, 14
Bateman, — (Miss), 10
Beck, Dorothy Dayton, *66*
Bell, James Ford, *152*; 152
Benson, Vernon, 100, 132–33
Berlis, — (Mr.), 145
Birkett, David, 70
Black Hills (SD), *195;* 194–95
Blair, David Dayton, *66*
Blair, Frederic, 152
Blair, Josephine Elizabeth (Mrs. Frederic) (26 Apr 1889–), *2, 66*; 7, 10, 13, 20, 63, 87, 125, 135, 152–53; Dayton's Dry Goods, 30, 60, 65, 124
Blaisdell, John T., 20
Bliss, Addie Corliss (Mrs. Cortis James), *190*; 24
Bliss, Cortis James (Rev.) (1861–1929), 24, 139
Bliss, Emma Gamble (Mrs. Cortis James) (–Aug 1892), 24
Bliss, Frank Hartsough (1887–1917), 24, 139
Bliss, Franklin, 24
Bliss, Grace (niece of Grace Caruthers Bliss Dayton) *184;* 181, 184, 190–91, 195, 198
Bliss, Grace Caruthers, *see* Dayton, Grace Caruthers Bliss
Bliss, Margaret Lawrence, 24
Bliss, Robert Woods, 24
Bliss, Tasker Howard (Gen.), 24
Bliss, Thomas, 23
Bliss Genealogy, A, 22, 25, 28, 184
Bloomingdale's, NYC, 46
Boddy, (Dr. William), 145
Borlaug, Norman, 95
Boulder Bridge Farm Co., *96–97, 99, 114*; 94–98, 108, 113–18, 132, 139, 183, 205; horses (including Belgians), *116–17*; 97, 108–109, 117, 131, 133; dairy

Index

herd, *114–15*; 107, 114–15; gardening, 186; incorporation; livestock (including Guernseys), *114*; 96–97, 106, 113–17, 118; poultry, 115; sheep, 109; sold, 118; Sunday lunches, 123; swine, 115

Boy Scouts, 59

Brown, Earle, *110*; 109–111

Bull, Dan, 135

Chadwick, Emma, *see* Dayton, Emma Chadwick

Chapman, Joe, 71, 77

Chase, Helen Louise Hayden, *66*

Crosby, Franklin M., *146*; 145

Crosby, John, 145

Country Life, 95

Curtiss, Glenn, *40*; 40; airplane, 40, 54

Dalrymple, Bernice (Mrs. John), 183, 186

Dayton, Betsy, 198

Dayton, Brandt, 178

Dayton, Bruce Bliss (16 Aug 1918) *57, 66, 100–102, 120, 126, 129, 197, 208, 213*; 22, 46, 67, 96, 102–105, 114, 121–22, 128, 134–35, 138, 141, 147, 151, 178, 188, 203; Blake School, 130; clubs/organizations, 186, 212; Dayton Co., positions, 174, 204–205, 212; director, Northwest National Life Ins. Co., 111; equestrian competition, 105, 194; family, 178, 215; military service, 151, 162, 174; sports, 132; Univ. of MN, honorary doctorate of law, 212; Yale Univ., 91, 117, 123, 133, 145, 161

Dayton, Caroline Ward, *see* Hayden, Caroline Dayton

Dayton, David Day (–3 Aug 1881), 4, 122

Dayton, David Draper, Jr., *66*

Dayton, Donald Chadwick (13 Aug 1914–22 Jun1989), *57, 66, 100–102, 120, 126, 129, 160, 208, 213*; 92, 96, 102, 103, 122, 128, 141, 144, 147; 4-H member, 105; Blake School, 111, 130; clubs/organizations, 211; Dayton Co., positions, 159–61, 163–64, 167, 169, 175, 204–205, 211; death, 211; family, 178, 215; Nicollet Mall, 211; polio, 130, 132; retirement, 211; sports, 132; Yale Univ., 117, 133; *see also* Okabena Co.

Dayton, Douglas James (2 Dec 1924–6 Jul 2013), *100–103, 105, 120, 125–26, 129, 131, 134, 205, 213*; 96, 102–104, 122, 141, 144; Amherst College, 133, 174; Blake School, 130; clubs/organizations, 212; Dade, Inc., 212; Dayton Co., 205; Dayton Hudson Corp., 212; family, 215; military service, 162–64; sports, 132

Dayton, Draper (David Draper) (13 Jun 1880–25 Jul1923), *2, 34, 64*; 3, 5, 7–8, 10, 20, 35–39, 49, 60, 63, 69, 138, 155; Dayton's Dry Goods (later The Dayton Co.) positions, 30, 42, 44–45, 63; death, 63–64; memorial tablet, *67*; military service, 174; Princeton Univ.,

Index

13, 15, 20, 22, 34, 133
Dayton, Edward, 178
Dayton, Elizabeth (24 May 1915–24 May 1915), 128
Dayton, Emma Chadwick (Mrs. George Draper) (–1931), *4, 66*; 3, 14, 20–21, 99, 121, 123–24, 134; boarders, 9; church activities/offices, 5–6, 8, 144, 154; 50th Anniversary, *84*; 83, 135
Dayton, George II, 208
Dayton, George Draper (1856–18 Feb 1938, age 80), *4, 14, 66*; 3, 4, 10, 33, 35, 38–39, 41–42, 44, 49, 52, 56, 63, 75–76, 80, 121–23, 153, 155, 167, 204; 50th Anniversary, *84*; 83, 135; 80th birthday, 92; *Autobiography*, 135; church activities/offices, 5–6, 15, 144–45, 154; Dayton's Dry Goods, 30, 65, 67; death, 92; estate, 126; land purchases, 15; move to Minneapolis, 16, 19; organizations, 147, 154; philanthropy, 154; realtor, 5; school board, 4; telephone, 14; *see also* Bank of Worthington
Dayton, George Draper, II, *66*; Princeton Univ., 81
Dayton, Grace Caruthers Bliss (Mrs. George Nelson) (15 Feb 1890–1 Apr 1966), *23, 25, 27, 66, 101–102, 126, 137, 180, 182, 184–85, 190, 196–97, 199–201, 213*; 22, 33, 75, 95–96, 100, 103, 126, 179, 181, 203–204, 214; bequests, 200–201, 208; Blake Corporation, 187; church activities, 28, 121, 145, 154, 183; clubs/organizations, 127, 183, 187, 190; community service award, 156, 178–79, 186; Dakota Wesleyan Univ., *187*; 23, 26–27, 183, 186; Dayton Foundation, 183; family, 139; descendants, 215; Granelda (cabin), 136; home in Florida; Red Cross project, 165, 182, 184–85; travels, 191–95; Wildflower Garden, *189*; 188–89; will, 199–200; *see also* Granelda Foundation; Residences
Dayton, George Nelson (called Neson), *see* Dayton, Nelson
John, 178
Dayton, Josephine Elizabeth, *see* Blair, Josephine Elizabeth
Dayton, Judd, 141
Dayton, Julia Winton (Judy) (Mrs. Kenneth N.), 140–41, 144
Dayton, Kenneth Nelson (20 Jul 1922–19 Jul 2003), *66, 100–103, 120, 125–26, 129, 133–34, 195, 208, 213*; 22, 64–55, 96, 102–103, 119, 121–22, 139, 141, 147, 151, 210; Blake School, 130; clubs/organizations, 213; Dayton Co., positions, 175, 205, 212; Dayton Hudson Corp., positions, 212; military service, 162, 174; family, 215; sports, 132; Yale Univ., 133
Dayton, Leonard V., *66*
Dayton, Lucy (daughter of Bruce), 181, 197–98
Dayton, Lucy (Mrs. Donald), *213*
Dayton, Mark (Gov.), 154, 178, 201

Index

Dayton, Mary Lee Lowe (Mrs. Wallace C.), *199*; 137, 140, 143–44, 178, 183, 194–96, 198–99, 208

Dayton, Nelson (George Nelson) (3 Aug 1886–1 Apr 1950), *frontispiece, 2, 6, 18, 57, 62, 66, 74, 98, 101, 108, 112, 120, 126, 158, 202*; 3–4, 7–8, 10, 13, 33, 49, 56, 60, 63–65, 69, 75, 106, 113, 122, 126, 214; Abbott Hospital, 145; bicycle, 12; church activities, 11, 20, 28, 143–46, 154; clubs/organizations, 13–14, 51, 71, 75, 81, 132, 135, 146–48, 150–54, 165; community service award, 156, 178–79, 186; courtship/wedding, 26, 28; Dayton's Dry Goods (later The Dayton Co.) positions, 30, 42–46, 70–71, 74, 76, 89, 121, 124, 159; death, 118, 156, 179; essay, 11–12; descendants, 215; Granelda (cabin), 136; humor, 135; illness, 174–76; international telephone call, 62, 81; liquor, 135; loans, 91; Macalester College, 21; military service, 147; philanthropy, 154; politics, 149; retirement, 174; stocks, 67; Univ. of Minnesota, 22; will, 178, 203–204; work for Alex Wilson, 13, 16, 19–20; *see also* Boulder Bridge Farm; Farms; Granelda Foundation; Okabena Co.; Residences

Dayton, Sally, 140, 178

Dayton, Wallace Corliss (12 Mar 1921–27 Oct 2002), *66, 100–103, 120, 125–26, 129, 134, 208, 213*; 96, 102–103, 122, 136–37, 141, 194–95; Amherst College, 133, 212; Blake School, 130; clubs/organizations, 211–12; Dayton Co., positions, 175, 205, 211–12; family, 215; military service, 162, 174; sports, 132; Target, positions, 212

Dayton, Ward W., *66*

Dayton Block (medical building), Minneapolis, 10, 19

Dayton Company, The, *32, 86, 91, 177, 207*; 33; 44th anniversary, 165; advertising, 46, 48, 53–54, 57, 67, 79, 130, 165, 172; air-conditioning, 90; air delivery service, 54; annex, *45*; 42, 44–45; anniversaries, 56, 79, 80–81, 91; appliance department, *175*; Aquatennial, 173–74; B. Dalton Books, 205; boat delivery service, *55*; Brides Bureau, *172*; 172–73; Brookdale, 111, 205; Budget Shop, 161; building schematic, *168*; candy kitchen, *58*; construction, 50, 56, 161; customer service, 54; Daisy Sale, 86, 164; delivery building, 167; delivery wagons, *43, 55*; 54; Downstairs Store (earlier basement store), 39–40, 50, 53, 70, 73, 83, 86; education, 52; employee benefits, 88; expansion, 40–41, 44, 47, 90, 159, 167; facility size, 83, 90; Fantle's purchase, 205; fashion designers, 170; finance loans, 164; fire, *49*; 48–49, 89; foot traffic, 81; fundraiser, 171; furniture department, 167; J. B. Hudson Co., 83, 89, 160, 168; *Jubilee!*,

223

58, 75, 164; Looking Glass Salon, 73, 167; Marshall Field's purchase, 205; men's furnishings, *77*; 75; Mervyn's purchase, 205; Milk Counter, *107*; name change, 42; newsletter (*The Daytonews, The Dayton News*), 53, 56–58, 76, 83, 89, 176; Oak Grille restaurant, *176*; Oriental rug department, 87; Oval Room (earlier called French Room, Model Room), *170*; 73, 167–71; parking garage, *82*; 83, 90; personnel, 77, 86, 88–89, 128; profit sharing, 52; profits, 86, 154, 175; radio programming, 59, 78; Red Cross projects, 184; reserves, 84, 167; Ridgedale, 205; Rosedale, 205; sales/revenues, 56–58, 81, 86, 91, 161, 176, 206–207; service philosophy, 71; shoe department, 50; sign on roof, 165; silk stocking sales event, 166; Sky Room, *169*; 167; social events, 53; Southdale, 205; staff training, 74; stock dividends/sales, 65–66, 72, 155, 204; stockholders, 90; Sunday restrictions, 177; Studio (interior design), 73, 173; Sub-Deb Shop, 73; Snow Fun/Sun Fun division, *162*; 161;Tea Room, 90, 106–108, 115; teamsters, 88–89; Town & Country department, 161; University (of MN) Store, *79–80*; 78, 205; warehouse, 167; window displays, *68*, *85, 171, 174*; *see also* Target Corp.

Dayton Family charts, 122, 215

Dayton Foundation (later Dayton Hudson Foundation), 87, 90, 121, 123, 152, 154–55, 196, 210

Dayton Hudson Corp. (DHC), 210, 212

Dayton Hudson Foundation, 155, 210

Dayton's Department Store (later The Dayton Corp., then Dayton Hudson Corp.), 16, 30, 210

Dayton's Dry Goods Co., *36–37*, *41*; 22, 30, 32, 36–37; name change, 42; remodeling, 39

Dayton Investment Co., 30

Denman, Louise Winchell Dayton, 66

Deutsche, Bill, 102

Dillman, W. A., *69*; 69, 174

Dobson, John, 151

Dobson, Weaver, 151, 153

Donaldson, L. S. (–1924), 71–72

Donaldson, L. S., & Co., 35, 42, 46, 54, 56, 58, 69, 81; expansion, 39, 41, 50; sold to Allied Stores Corp., 78

Donaldson, William, 15

Dow, Wallace Leroy, 7

Dry Goods Economist, 37

Dunwoody Institute, 59

Fantle's, Sioux Falls, SD, 205

Farms, Dayton-Bond Farm, 4; hay-barn fire, 5; horses, 97; garden, 101; Oak Leaf Farm, 22, 30, 60; sheep, 13; swine, 21; trees, 101; *see also* Boulder Bridge Farm

Filene, Lincoln, 46

Filene's, Boston, 46

First Methodist Episcopal Church, Mitchell, SD, 28

Index

First National Bank of Minneapolis, 42
Foreign Missions, 10
Fort Sneilling, 147

Gavin, Dorothy, 161
General Mills, 130
Gimbel, — (Mr.), 75
Gimbel-Zimmer Co., 50
Goodfellow's Dry Goods (later Dayton Dry Goods Co.), 15, 22, 32–33, 35; display window, *35*
Granelda Foundation, 155, 183, 200, 209
Great Depression, 84–87, 90, 92, 136, 147, 159, 205

Hayden, Caroline Dayton ("Miss Carrie") (5 Feb 1883–), *2, 66*; 3, 7, 14, 22, 87, 123, 125, 135, 145; Dayton's Dry Goods, 30, 60, 65, 124; dividends, 71; Wellesley College, 16, 20
Hayden, William Frederick, *66*
Hendricks family, 28
Heneman, Avis Louise Dayton, *66*
Higby, — (Mrs.), 186
Hill, Marie Thompson, 73
Hillis, — (Dr.), 14
Holidays, Arbor Day, 10; Christmas, *72*; 48, 73, 140, 198; Halloween, 13; Jul 4, 11–12, 15, 135; Thanksgiving, 79
Hotel Radisson, 173
Hudson's, Detroit, 46–47, 205
Huff, Bill, 179

International Livestock Show, 114

J. B. Hudson Co. (later JB Jewelers), *see* Dayton Co.
Johnson, Jeff, 189
Jones, — (Farmer), 13
Jones, — (Fish), 73
Jones, George, 48
Judd, Walter (U.S. Rep.), 187, 190

Kjome, Olaf, 98–99, 118

L. S. Donaldson & Co., *see* Donaldson, L. S., & Co.
Lake Vermilion, 136
Larsen, E. S., 87, 141, 153
Larson, C. J., *70*; 50, 65, 70, 72–73, 85, 173
Larson, G. L., 174
Long, Dalt, 99
Longfellow Gardens, 73
Longyear, Edmund J., 95–96
Loudon, George, 33
Lowe, Arnold (Rev.), *199*; 143, 196
Ludlow, Burr, 136
Luker, John, 65, 70

Macalester College, 21
Mann, Lloyd, 109
Marshall Field's, Chicago, 169, 205
Marshall Messenger, 8
May Department Stores Co., The, 75, 79, 205
May, — (Mr.), 78
McDonald, Angus, 116
McDermott, Edward, 203
Mervyn's, 205
Minneapolis, Aquatennial, 173; Chamber of Commerce, 210–11; First Presbyterian Church, 20; land purchases, 15; organizations,

Index

146–47; streets, 15, 48; Westminster Presbyterian Church, *16, 142, 209*; 20, 33, 81, 144, 179, 196, 208–209

Minneapolis Journal, 19, 34, 39, 42, 44, 48, 83

Minneapolis Retailers Assn., 51, 70, 146, 147

Minneapolis Star, 118, 156, 179

Minneapolis Symphony Orchestra (later Minnesota Orchestra), 79

Minnesota, Centennial, 186; Department of Natural Resources, 137; Governor's Residence, 154, 210; Landscape Arboretum, 188–89

Minnesota Loan & Investment Co., 4

Minnesota State Fair, 54, 105

Minnetonka Country Club, 132

Minnetonka Record, 119

Morse-Kahn, Deborah, 22

Mosher, J. B., 33

Nelson, Harry (Rev.), 4

Nelson, William S. (Rev.) 4, 154

New England Mutual Life Ins. Co., 90

New York Life Ins. Co., 47

New York State, 3

Nobles County, 4

Northwest Bancorporation (later Norwest, Wells Fargo), 147, 166

Northwestern National Bank, 147

Office of Price Administration (OPA), 164

Okabena Co., The, 138–39, 179

Page, L. S., 106

Parmeter, W. E. (Roy), 70, 89

Per-Lee, John, *70*; 65, 70, 173

Pets, 12, 102–103, 105

Phillips, Alan, *69*; 47, 70

Pillsbury, — (Mrs.), 133

Pillsbury, Alfred, 151

Pillsbury, Jane, 133

Pillsbury, John S. (Gov., 1827–1901), 20

Pillsbury, John S., Jr., *148*; 147

Piper, Harry, 46

Piper Jaffray, 46

Presbyterian Foundation for Home Missions, 146

Quinlan, Elizabeth, 168

Red Cross, 53

Residences, Boulder Bridge Farm, *97*; 95, 99, 101; Lake Minnetonka, 140; Long Lake, 140; Minneapolis, *29, 178*; 19–20, 28, 60, 138, 154, 177–78, 185, 194; Worthington, *7*; 4, 5, 7, 16

Retail Research Association (RRA), 46–47, 75, 76

Richardson, Bonney Blair, 66

Ridgedale, 205

Roosevelt, Franklin D. (U.S. Pres.), 147

Rose family, 8

Rosedale, 205

Sears Roebuck, 77, 205

Skinner, H. S., 174

Smallwood, Charlie, 16

Smallwood, Florence Moulton (Mrs.), 16

Southdale, 205
Sports, 102, 130, 150
Stacy, Ima Winchell, 52
Stassen, Harold E. (Gov.), *149*; 149–50
Stone, Jackson M., 95
Strawbridge & Clothier, Philadelphia, 46; advertisement, 81

Target Corp., 155, 205, 211
Target Foundation (earlier Dayton Foundation, Dayton Hudson Foundation, Granelda Foundation), 155
Thune, Christine, *127*; 100, 128, 141
Thorpe Brothers, 9
Travels/vacations, 13–14, 123, 126, 191

Unemployment, 87
U.S. War Industries Board, 53
University of Minnesota, *see* Dayton's University Store

Van Dewlap, John R., 42

Wakefield, Lyman, 164
Ward, Harold, *112*
Ward, Laysha, 155, 211

WBAH radio, 59
Webber, Dick, 47, 191
Webber, Oscar, 47, 191–94
Wells, Stuart, 168–69
Westminster Presbyterian Church, *see* Minneapolis; Worthington
White, Arthur C., *69*; 47, 69, 89, 174
Wilson, Alex, 13, 16
Wilson, Leslie V. (Les.), *98*; 98–99, 106, 108–109, 117–18
Wilson, "Tana Jim," 98
Women, employment, 51
Woodhill Country Club, 85
Woodworth, Harry, 113–14, 116–17
World War I, 45, 50, 53, 54, 59, 182
World War II, 130, 138, 162–66
Worthington, 3, 15, 140; Board of Trade, 4; Clary Addition, 5–6; Lake Okabena, 8; Westminster Presbyterian Church, 5, 11, 15, 143; *see also* Bank of Worthington
Worthington Advance, 4, 5, 13, 14
Worthington Globe, 11, 14

The main text of this book is set in 12-point Adobe Garamond Pro; other type blocks are set in variations of that typeface. The text stock is McCoy 80-lb Matte Text. The endsheets are of 80-lb Rainbow® Briar Text. The cloth edition is bound in Arrostox Blue Ribbon B-Cloth; the dustjacket stock is McCoy 100-lb Gloss Text. The leather version is bound in goatskin. Both editions have gold-foil stamp.

Design/production:	E. B. Green Editorial, St. Paul, Minnesota
Text & jacket layout:	Ken Green, St. Paul, Minnesota
Indexing:	Patricia Green, Homer, Alaska
Printing:	Sexton Printing Inc., St. Paul, Minnesota
Binding:	Midwest Editions, Minneapolis (clothbound)
	Campbell-Logan Bindery, Inc., Minneapolis (leatherbound with slipcase)